HOW TO WAKE UP SINGING

BROADMAN PRESS / *Nashville, Tennessee*

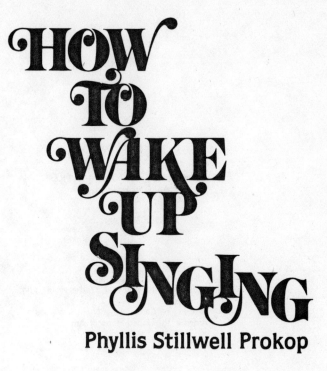

HOW TO WAKE UP SINGING

Phyllis Stillwell Prokop

Dewey Decimal Classification: 248.4
Subject heading: CHRISTIAN LIFE // SPIRITUAL LIFE

Library of Congress Card Catalog Number: 79-50877
Printed in the United States of America.

PREFACE

The title of this book was not chosen lightly. It came about in this way: I have a friend who recently went through an unhappy and trying divorce. She moved through the months of tension and resettlement with great dignity and outward calm, but from little things she said and little responses she made I was very much aware of the sadness she was carrying.

After a time as I felt that she was appearing more contented both mentally and emotionally I asked her, "Lynda, do you think you are all over it?"

She answered with only a small catch in her voice, "Yes, I think I'm over it, but sometimes late in the night I wake up crying."

Her words stayed with me week after week, and then I realized that we are all trying to avoid this poignant situation which she described; in fact, what we all want is the exact opposite—we want to Wake Up Singing.

This book, therefore, is directed toward the discovery of How to Wake Up Singing through the development of a singing state of mind based on biblical principles.

The book comes from a conviction that singing is good, singing is possible, and singing is authorized by God. Singing is a way of waking up and it is a way of going to sleep. This book is concerned with the techniques for developing the songs which last for a lifetime.

CONTENTS

Dedicated to
Authors Unltd. of Houston
who have given to me constant
encouragement, generous assistance,
and enough joy to make singing
inevitable

Introduction

The life of the mind and emotions is in some respects as fragile as a summer cloud. Each soft breeze of conversation or sun ray of smile alters its shape and tint in passing. We are indeed vulnerable creations.

We are not, however, as defenseless as the cloud. We have the ability to consider and decide on the shape to which we will ultimately conform and the length of time we will stand where the sun rays strike us.

This book is designed to help us look at our own fragile beings with a clear eye and find some techniques which can help us to be shaped and warmed so we may live more consistently and with a contented state of mind.

Often this look requires us to question attitudes or experiences which are shading our days, and in this book each chapter deals with a separate questioning or solution technique for dealing with one aspect of experience. Each chapter says, "This is another way of looking at a portion of your day. This is a specific technique which will help you discover *How to Wake Up Singing*."

1

Pray a Prayer Which Can Be Answered Today

Not all prayers can reasonably be answered in a single day. Some prayers may be for long-term developments such as a continuing request that our country will be at peace, or that we, our husbands or wives, or our children will mature effectively both spiritually and physically. These are not prayers to which a definite answer can be anticipated in one day. They are involved with lifetime progressions. But all prayers do not fall into this category.

There are many prayers which are for today, and today only, such as:

> a prayer for wisdom in a business arrangement which must be completed today
>
> a prayer for definite evidence of improvement in an illness
>
> a prayer for the confidence to perform well in a specific sales presentation
>
> a prayer for the ability to perform well on an examination
>
> a prayer that your work will be handled advantageously
>
> a prayer for encouragement in a trying situation
>
> a prayer for patience with children
>
> a prayer for the ability to present your talents well
>
> a prayer to be free from fear in a stress situation
>
> a prayer for wise words in a social or business meeting
>
> a prayer for graciousness in a tense situation
>
> a prayer for guidance in making an investment

a prayer for clear thought in making a decision

a prayer for discernment in a life choice

By rewording each of these requests, we will probably find that they can be applied to the circumstances of our own lives at this moment. We may not be giving a sales presentation today, but we may be giving a program for a church or neighborhood group. We may not be considering making a lifetime decision, but we may be considering an investment. Whatever the details, the thought is the same. Decisions and actions will be accomplished today. They will be completed in twelve hours. By the time we go to bed tonight we will have a yes or no response to some of these events. Such immediate happenings are possible subjects for the prayer which we can pray today and for which we can anticipate an answer today.

Not only will we have the joy of seeing prayers answered but also very definite results will arise from such a method of prayer.

First, we will find fellowship with God deepening daily. Fellowship is a shared experience; even as we treasure the experience, God also treasures our coming to him for fellowship. This is evident from the constant invitations of the Bible to come to God. To mention only one, he says, "Call unto me, and I will answer thee, and shew thee great and mighty things, which thou knowest not" (Jer. 33:3). This verse offers the assurance of God's answers in response to our simply coming to him with our requests! Elsewhere he invites us to come to him with every request and thereby avoid all anxiety about our problems. He says:

Be careful for nothing; but in every thing by prayer and supplication with thanksgiving let your requests be made known unto God.

And the peace of God, which passeth all understanding, shall keep your hearts and minds through Christ Jesus (Phil. 4:6-7).

Second, we will build a discipline of prayer into our lives by establishing a daily pattern of praying about a problem which is causing us anxiety and worry. This discipline will make it easy for us to enter into conversation with God. This system of sharing with him the problem which is uppermost in our minds for today, will provide a specific topic around which fellowship will thrive.

Did you ever attempt to visit with someone with whom you had nothing in common? I was once stranded with an electrical repairman in an elevator which was stuck between floors in a downtown building. This man was totally wrapped up in his only area of interest—electrical repair. He was obviously skilled and able, but electricity was his only interest. At first this interest seemed to make him a fortunate companion since he might be able to correct the problem with the elevator. Later, however, he was unable to do this. We shouted back and forth until we were convinced that others in the building were working on the problem of our stuck elevator. We stood in the small closet-like space waiting to be released and attempted to visit.

For a few minutes we discussed the weather, the possibilities of repairing the elevator, and after that the conversation ground down to a halt. I found myself with one of the few people I have ever seen who only had one interest to discuss. This man had no interest in discussing his family, ideas, recreation, church, books, newspapers, or any of the dozens of things which seemed to me to be general conversational topics.

I can only say this, we had very poor fellowship in our thirty-minute period of imprisonment together. After about fifteen minutes of standing, we sat down in the floor side by side with our feet stretched out in front of us. In such close quarters, he lectured to me about electrical controls. I listened. I will readily admit that I learned a few things about that topic. I will also say that this was not one of the high hours of experience of my life for the simple reason that my companion and I had no immediate topic of mutual interest to discuss.

Perhaps if we had been there two hours instead of thirty minutes, we would have eventually discovered that we both enjoyed collecting barbed wire or even that we both had a weakness for James Thurber. As it was, no such breakthrough was made.

Such poverty of fellowship as I knew in the elevator will never be present with the Lord in the life of the individual who comes to God each day with a specific prayer and who sees that specific prayer develop through the day and come to its conclusion as darkness falls. Where there is good conversation each morning and anticipation of a shared experience of request and answer, there will be deep friendship. God has said come, so each morning we may go and take with us the topic which presses for an answer that day.

Third, the result of praying the daily answerable prayer is that faith will develop before our amazed eyes. The fact that God will reach his hand into the little problems of our days is a constant miracle. The comprehension of that miracle will glow, simmer, and explode in the mind with shattering force. One day the thought will overpower us and we will tremble as we say, "God, you do hear my little prayers and you do answer them immediately."

God does not restrict us to a single prayer per day. He has not said, I will allocate one answer to you today. This is, indeed, not the point. The point is that the one answered prayer per day is the minimum; it is the beginning place; it is the starting line. After that the number of prayers may grow. The one answerable prayer for the day is simply a system for reminding us that today God is at work in our lives and ready to answer the most needed prayer of our present existence.

An incident which occurred when I was in college probably laid the groundwork for my fascination with the thought of a daily, effective prayer. The school day had been long and tiring, and as I left the campus I decided to drop by the home of the mother of one of my friends. I had gone there many evenings to enjoy a half-hour of conversation and relaxation over a cup of hot tea.

I was surprised to find my friend's mother, and surely she was my friend also, seated in her living room with a letter in her hands and tears in her eyes. She told me that the letter contained the news of the death of her aunt.

After I had expressed my sympathy, she said quite simply, "Actually, I hardly knew my aunt, and yet already I feel her loss. Something has gone out of my life." She continued to talk of her relationship with this elderly lady whom she scarcely knew and yet whom she missed.

She told me that on her twelfth birthday she had received a greeting from her aunt. With the greeting had come these words: "Along with my wishes for a happy day, I also send a promise to you. I send the promise that each day, as long as I live, I will pray for your peace, happiness, and success for that one day."

My friend went on to tell me that as the years had passed and she had grown from a twelve-year-old child into an adult—a mother of college-age children, that she had faced numberless difficult days with the happy realization that her aunt had already preceded her in that day with a prayer for her well-being.

My friend had reason to feel sad at the death of her aunt. She had indeed lost something very wonderful. She had lost someone who would pray in her behalf each and every day for that specific day.

This is an example of someone who prayed for another person each day. Now let me tell you how the daily answerable prayer pattern developed in my life. I discovered long ago that my contentment and peace of mind are deeply involved and enmeshed in my writing experience. On the days I write I feel fulfilled and at peace; the days I do not make the time for writing, I finish my day vaguely defeated and ill at ease with myself.

However, there are many days when reading back over my writing, I discover that the work is poor. I have obviously failed to express what I had wished to say. This is certainly no unique experience; rather it is the experience of most writers as well as workers in any craft; every day is not a day of fine accomplishment. Since the writing experience is so much a part of my life, I decided to make that activity a matter of definite daily prayer, the prayer for that day.

The first day I tried it, I asked that I would be able to write five, usable, worthwhile pages during that morning's work. I plunged into my work as usual. Suddenly I found myself moving along, the words coming easily, the thoughts moving in orderly fashion, and a deep contentment growing in my mind. There was neither tension nor frustration; I was truly working.

I wrote a first draft and then edited and retyped my work, and then I took the pages from my typewriter and placed them in order to give them a final editing. Then my eye picked up the number in the upper right-hand corner of the page. It said page five. I had asked the Lord for the ability to write five competent pages that morning, and he had answered my simple request. This was a truly spiritual experience for me. I had asked; he had heard; he had answered, and the answer was the answer I needed for that specific day. A finished book did not miraculously appear on my desk. No, indeed. Instead, I had been blessed with the ability and concentration to live my day effectively. Expand that thought into a thousand todays and tomorrows, and the result is an effective life.

PRAY A PRAYER

There is a verse which emphasizes the todayness of need and the todayness of help. It says, "Call upon me in the day of trouble: I will deliver thee, and thou shalt glorify me" (Ps. 50:15). If we handle the trouble and the need of each day, it is handled for our entire lives. We have only today. As the prayer of today and for today is asked and answered, we grow closer to God, and closeness to him is the place for waking up singing.

2
Fight for Your Life

God created the miracle of life. He gave each of us a slice of it, a slice approximately seventy years wide and as deep as we care to make it. He placed this miracle in a context of dawns, sunsets, high noons, and midnights. He gave all of this to us without cost. Below are some of the statements I have heard in the past year about this miraculous gift of life.

"Life doesn't seem to mean much to me anymore."
"My life is just one endless routine."
"I can't seem to get any joy out of living."
"My life is totally empty."
"I seem to have no place in this life."
"I have lost my way."
"I haven't had a really good day in months."
"My life is drudgery."
"I have to have a drink during the day just to endure life."
"I have to take tranquilizers to give me a sense of well-being."
"I wish I could escape my way of life."

Are these reactions to a miracle? Are these reactions to the greatest gift ever known?

As I look back over these statements, various faces come into focus. They are the faces of the people who made these despairing remarks. One face is that of a prominent businessman; another is the face of a lovely housewife and hostess. These are neither foolish nor cowardly people. They

19

are people who are functioning in a successful manner in some area. They are moving through life in a way we are inclined to admire and applaud. But down deep they are crying, "I wish I could escape!"

Suddenly, as we hear the cry, we may realize that at times in our lives we have cried with them. We have also wished to escape the lives we know. Even if our wish has only remained for a short moment, we suddenly know that the "they" who have not understood and appreciated life have suddenly become the "we" who have not understood, appreciated, and I will add, have not relished life.

Again I ask why this situation exists? Why do they, why do we, at times wish to escape life with a cry in our throats, "My life is drudgery." Something must be wrong, and it is. But what is wrong?

What is wrong is that we have never learned to fight for this wonderful life we have been given. Instead, we stand back and wait for life to come to us, bringing its beauty in its outreached hands; we have never even learned that we must step forward to receive it.

We have not learned that much of life is an adversary situation in which we need to oppose misconceptions and foolish decisions which are our worst foes. These are our enemies. They are, in fact, enemies which we must destroy in order to gain strength to move on to greater victories over ourselves as well as over destructive exterior forces. We need to learn who and what these daily enemies are that plunge us into despair, and we need to know how to defend ourselves against their attacks. The enemies conceal themselves well amid our confusions and muddled thinking, but here are a few of their names. They are more easy to identify once we have a hint as to their shapes and forms.

lack of imagination
lack of dynamics

old superstitions and sayings
refusal to make plans
fear for personal security
lack of observation
muddled thinking
other people

In fact, anything which blocks the path to a good life can be described as an enemy of life.

Many of these enemies are permanent or long-term enemies rather than crisis opponents. They have not appeared in a sudden moment of time in a disaster situation; instead, they have been a part of our lives for years, gaining strength by feeding on our imagined inadequacies and our unwillingness to oppose them. They are, in general, slowly developing traits of lack of enthusiasm and loss of touch with reality.

Most of the people who made the negative statements which were listed at the beginning of the chapter were not in crisis situations, they were on the even highway of life. "My life is totally empty," was spoken by a woman who had no major problem facing her. She simply had forgotten how to fight for daily life. Her story was this:

Diane was a thirty-five-year-old widow who had worked most of her life. After the death of her husband, she continued to work at her same job and to live in the same house they had shared for fifteen years.

She told me on several occasions that no one ever invited widows to their homes for dinner or out for special events. She did not add, however, that she never invited anyone over for dinner. She never arranged an evening out, or called to see if others would like to join her.

This situation of complaining withdrawal typified her general attitude. She had pulled back into her home where she lived in self-imposed solitude, venturing out only to go to work where she spent her days among people she had known for years and yet had never incorporated into her life in any way.

She neither planned for little happinesses of life nor did she expect them. In short, she did not fight for life. She accepted the meager crumbs which came without effort and then complained of her total emptiness.

Let me contrast this with the life of a friend who learned early to fight the little battles with charm and determination. Betty married a man who refused to work to support her and their children. After some five years of struggling to support the five of them with her salary, she divorced her husband. She was a beautiful woman who had been a model, and she had much attention; however, she decided not to remarry until the children were grown.

She began to build a satisfying and rich a life as she was able. She developed a pleasant social life and attended the numerous stimulating events available in her city. By sharing her life with her mother, both the good events (such as raises in salary and the pleasant activities) as well as the discouragements, she was able to add to both their lives as she contributed excitement and achievement to her mother's life and her mother in turn helped her with the children.

In this action alone, she displayed an unusually gracious and self-rewarding system, as she avoided the pitfall of sharing only misery with the people who surrounded her in a home situation. It is frequently easy to cry out and complain against the lacks and keep the good things to ourselves.

The years have passed. Betty now has grown children, and a continuing, vital life.

The similarities and differences in the lives of Diane and Betty are evident in that each suffered a trauma in her life. Both lost their husbands and were forced to reshape their lives. The difference is that Betty was willing to fight for life, while Diane surrendered without a struggle.

Dylan Thomas, the Welsh poet, spoke probably one of the most telling words of advice about the approach of old age when he wrote the poem, "Do Not Go Gentle into That Good Night." His advice is applicable to all of life. He could have said, do not go without a struggle into any empty and unsatisfying darkness of life. Fight for life! Oppose anything which robs life of the glory it was intended to have!

I have used the word *fight*, and this word suggests an enemy. The enemies are real, but we often skillfully conceal their faces from our own eyes. Perhaps it is too painful to admit that they are present within us.

I have suggested a partial, very incomplete list of enemies who need to be opposed if we are to live with joy. There are so many more, both interior and exterior, enemies which will come to your mind. But first let's look at some of these foes listed above who live inside each of us and constantly threaten to take the reins of our lives if we do not contend with them effectively.

Lack of Imagination

One of the definitions of *imagination* is the possibility of producing ideal creations consistent with reality. This is the type of imagination we are thinking of. Before any of us can strive for something beautiful and worthwhile, we must be able to imagine that it exists; we must be able to visualize it. The young lady who can only visualize herself working on the most menial level is unlikely to rise much higher than the level she sees in her mind. The young man who sees himself as living in a slum surrounded by degradation is unlikely to leave that slum and try for better conditions. The picture must exist in the mind before the individual can strive for it.

We may not share the problem of either the menial or the slum dweller, but we may have climbed to only a slightly higher level and settled down there without a struggle, never fighting for a dream or a hope for rising higher. The lack of dream, the lack of hope, lack of imagining better things— this is the enemy to be opposed if we are to fight for life.

The Bible says it best in the words: "Where there is no vision, the people perish" (Prov. 29:18). But it is very easy to relate this Scripture only to unusual events or lofty group activities. We may applaud the words heartily if we think of the vision to build a new church or feed the starving people of a famine area. However, we may turn from it blindly when it concerns our own daily lives. When the matter at stake is our own question about opening a shop, accepting a challenging job, or even something as simple as inviting new friends over for dinner, we may accept lack of vision and lack of imagination as our method of operation without even giving it a second look. We may fail to realize that small daily vision is also important and, in fact, referred to equally by the Scripture. There is no yardstick put on the vision.

Lack of Dynamics

Some people enter the days as though they were constant holidays. Others drag through the days as though they are marching to muffled drums. Paul instructed the Colossians about the manner of moving into their days when he said, "Whatsoever ye do, do it heartily, as unto the Lord" (Col. 3:23). This is a picture of action and determination. This is the attitude of dynamic force which brings about accomplishment and the pride of accomplishment. Lack of dynamic force is a recognizable enemy to be faced in toe-to-toe combat. The first step in combat is to discover the reason for lack of dynamics.

Is it boredom? Is it that you have never found anything worth being dynamic about? Do you lack confidence in the results of your dynamic activities? Do you lack confidence in your ability to be a part of a dynamic activity? Are you physically unable to participate dynamically?

Once you discover your reason for lack of force, the battle lines may be partially drawn. If lack of physical energy is your enemy, you need to talk with your doctor. But if boredom robs you of force, the first steps into battle are less obvious. Boredom, however, falls before new interests, new friends, new experiences with old friends, and an open mind to the world around you. A good rule of thought is the suggestion to participate even where there is no real interest until interest grows to encourage participation.

A dictionary definition of *boredom* is "to be wearied by dullness." (Have you ever read any more depressing words?) The opposite of this definition is to be dynamic by brightness. This opposite is what we are reaching for in our struggle. We go beyond the weariness as we reach for the stimulating and vital. We go beyond the empty hour of staring into space to a full hour of visiting with a friend about those things which bring her satisfaction; we go beyond the empty hour of brooding to seeking out a friend who satisfies our need for inspiration and information; we go beyond the empty hour of putting off jobs to the full hour of accomplishment.

These are some steps to personal dynamics, and there are many more. We each tailor the steps to our needs, our interests, our enthusiasm; we pursue that which is uniquely our own. At the end of the pursuit, we look in the mirror to see that we have become vigorous and dynamic.

Old Superstitions and Sayings

Studies have shown that many people depend on old sayings and superstitions as guides for their lives. Otherwise intelligent people may make decisions on the basis of nothing more valid than the words of a half-remembered motto.

The person who makes a decision against moving to a

new job by reminding himself that a "rolling stone gathers no moss," may be shaken when he considers the market value of moss. It is equally disquieting to decide whether, in fact, "out of sight is out of mind" or whether "absence makes the heart grow fonder." There is wisdom in many of the old sayings, but some are little more than a reflection of that particular stage of civilization in which the sayings were coined.

Whatever the source of the old sayings which may be tossed your way or which may come into your mind in hours of decision, it is wise to look at them very carefully. If they are no more than vague advice from some questionable source, they may be the enemy who needs to be conquered. They may represent a voice to which you have listened too long, the voice of superstition rather than the more firm voice of God and your own reasonable understanding.

During hours of stress and decisions, the mind is particularly vulnerable to any offers of help as it reaches out for firm footing upon which to base its next action. This is the reason the brief, remembered words seem so useful to the distressed person; they offer an instant word of advice in a time of needed help. Too often the advice is questionable, at best, and actually harmful at worst.

Refusal to Make Plans

Anyone who wishes to drift through life without really comprehending how wonderful living can be, can readily avail himself of the opportunity. Simply do not make any plans of any kind. Rely entirely on chance happenings and your drifting path is guaranteed.

Vigorless, misdirected, and wasted days are insured by a planless life. It is easy to see why this aimless drifting is difficult to identify as an enemy of life. It develops so slowly. We drift through one day and then another. Summer merges into fall and fall into winter, and eventually we discover that we have drifted through life. The enemy who directed our life and needed to be destroyed was the simple negative attitude toward plans.

Someone has pointed out that the perfectionist, who demands that every moment be planned and that the plan be carried out exactly as he sees it, has closed all doors to the unexpected happenings which are larger than his own anticipation. This is true, and certainly it is not this level of planning which we are seeking.

Instead we are thinking in terms of the planning process which expresses itself in goals, both long-range and short-range and which includes the planning for little events of special thought, special visits, special trips, special meals, special books, special purchases, special ceremonies, special parties, special lectures, and special anticipations, and I will add special answers to prayers.

Fear for Personal Security

Sophocles, who was born in 495 B.C. said, "To him who is in fear, everything rustles," and when we suddenly realize that everything is rustling, it is time to fight fear.

The fears of our life may go far beyond the fear of attacks and disaster; they may include fear of other's opinions, fear of new people and new places, or fear of defeat. Any one of these fears can destroy happiness in a life and suffocate joy. The fear of defeat or even the fear of appearing foolish can rule our participation in any new experiences. The first time we ice-skate or ride horseback we may look awkward, but why should we care? We could hardly expect to excel at anything in a few moments; how sad to miss whole worlds of experience only because we are afraid of someone looking at us. It has been said that the person who is afraid to try something because he may fail, already has. And I believe there is much wisdom here. Fear is the enemy of a full life. Fear deserves to be attacked and defeated.

Lack of Observation

It is possible to go through life and never observe the seasons, the new house being built on the next block, the dog that lives the third house from the corner, the new product in the grocery store, the girl with the violet eyes, or the book on the rack. One might not notice the width of the new coat lapels, the new word suddenly appearing in every newscaster's report, the expression on a friend's face, the price of every product whether you wish to buy it or not, the architecture of the courthouse, the color of the spring leaves, the month the robin returns to your state—to mention only a few.

The more wide-awake you are, the more you will observe, and the more you observe, the richer your life will be.

Some people are natural observers, and others are almost unaware of the world around them. There are a number of psychological tests available to discover just how much an individual is actually seeing, and the results may be startling to any of us who take such a test. According to the standard score, some people observe as much as 60 percent more than others. Just contrast the richness of living of the observer and the nonobserver. Think of the limitations of a life which is filled only with a few mundane work-a-day details, while the glory of the universe lies ignored.

It is true that some minds are so rich that they can take a very few physical details and from them create a world of deeply experienced reality. The poet Emily Dickinson was such a person. But this is truly another type of observation. It involves an intense awareness of emotion and response to closely surrounding events. But for most of us, the true colors of our lives are determined by our openness to our broad, physical, and mental worlds.

After we have agreed that there are differences in the richness of life of an observer and a nonobserver, the real question becomes, How does one increase his breadth and depth of observation? For a starting point, it is primarily a matter of developing interests.

Consider the case of a seamstress who works with cloth all day. She will find herself aware of the texture, weight, and feel of each kind of cloth. If you handed her a piece of satin or taffeta in total darkness, she could immediately identify it. The slub of a raw silk would be apparent to her observant fingers, and a smooth cotton would be completely identifiable. Why would all of this be true? The answer is that she is totally aware of the varying characteristics of cloths. She knows cloth. She is fascinated by cloth. She is open to all new information about cloth. She knows when a new cloth appears in the stores. She is conscious, and she is aware in this area.

The situation of the seamstress can be applied to any field. As we begin to know something about an area, we become observant of its details. We are all aware of the experience of learning a new word or expression and suddenly hearing and seeing this word everywhere. This is because we are now aware of the word. It was present before, but we were not open to it. It meant nothing to us, we did not know what it meant, so it was closed off from our experience. It is possible to close off the entire world by lack of interest in it. The world can be reduced to the size of our own personal problems, but what a meager and poor world that is! How many people do you know who have compressed the great, beautiful world into the size and shape of their own lives and then have wondered why life was not more interesting.

The first slow steps of becoming a more observant person

may be almost like those of a baby learning to walk. They may be very short steps characterized by surprise and uncertainty.

For example, to become observant of the plant growing beside your front door you may ask yourself if you know whether the plant is a ligustrum or a pittosporum. Do you know whether it will have berries in the fall or flowers in the spring? A new world begins to open when you decide to observe and observe again until you can say, "I have a pyracantha or fire thorn by my front door and it has beautiful reddish-orange berries in the fall and winter." Never again will the world of plants be closed to you, you will have started on your life of observation. It will lead you to new interests which will add new dimensions to your life. Someone has said that there is nothing as boring as a bored person, and this is of necessity, true. When we are bored we have nothing to share but boredom. But as we each develop interests in the world around us, all boredom leaves. How can we be bored in a world of exciting knowledge?

Charles, my husband, is a very observant person in many areas. He remembers every turn in a road, and highway numbers from highways we traveled on vacations years ago. When our boys were little, he fell into the habit of asking them casual questions about things they had seen while we were on a trip. When the children got back into the car he would casually ask, "Did you notice the brand of the plumbing fixtures in the restroom?" It became a game for the boys to observe and remember details. It soon was a matter of great pride for them to remember the names of motels, parks, scenic spots, and people we met along the way.

Nothing could have been of less significance than some of the facts they stored away, but they developed the invaluable skill of observing the thousands of small things around them. It became a way of thinking for them to look at and mentally catalog information. In short, the participation encouraged their observation skills. They are now both highly observant men who carry with them a wealth of interesting information about their worlds. I believe it is partially because they were methodically taught to be observant by a father who was interested in everything, even the brand of plumbing fixtures.

Perhaps your interests lie in the great events of history, antiques, beautiful parks and waterways of the world, great dress designers, beautiful homes, plants and growing things—whatever you observe, the principle is the same. The interest, the observation, is the vital component. It is the observation which makes the old world into a vitally new world for you whether it is the observation of the butterflies in the rain forests of South America or the shape of the raindrops which fall against your own windowpanes. But whatever the area of interest, there can be a continually expanding list of interests and observations in your life; and the days can become more and more exciting and vigorous.

Muddled Thinking

Before any of us can wake up singing there is one enemy who must be attacked. He is the enemy, muddled thinking. Half-truths, vague ideas, and shadowy impressions are more likely to come to our minds than good clear thought much of the time.

Let's look briefly at one of the very practical results of muddled thinking at work in our lives this moment. Try to answer this question clearly. What would you like to accomplish this year? If you have a clear statement to make about this, you are an unusual person. Most of us have a great wastebasket full of odds and ends of things we are thinking about, but any one clear statement of purpose evades us.

This one question of our plan for the year may not be any more important than our plans for the next hour or day, but it served to point out our lack of clear, orderly thought, even as we consider something as important as our futures.

I was recently stopped short with the realization that I frequently do not even make the effort to think what I really want to see happen in my life. I was taught a rich lesson in this area by a friend.

My friend was faced with the necessity for starting her life over. She talked with me a number of times about some possible alternatives of places to live, jobs, and so forth, and I found my mind was working entirely along lines of how to accomplish the number of possibilities she suggested. Then suddenly she said, "But really the question is not how at this point. The question is, what do I really want to do? What is the thing I would most want to see happen? What plan is the absolute first choice for my future? When I have made this decision," she went on, "then I will be ready to consider how to accomplish it."

There are always dozens of possible alternative actions in any given circumstance, and many of these actions can be accomplished with a minimum of effort. But that is not the point, that is only muddled thinking. The point is, as my friend said, "What is the absolute, the first desire of my heart and mind in the matter? What do I want to do most?" Until I know what I really want to do, I need not consider how to do it. If I do not know my desired direction how can I plot my course? All movement will need to be done over and over again until the aims are clarified.

My friend faced her decision and after this question of aims was answered she could start looking for ways to accomplish her aim. She was then on firm ground. She had clarified her muddled thinking and was ready to act. I was startled at how seldom I had thought this clearly. More often I had moved from one possible alternative to another, following events without ever really understanding my aim. There is a vast difference in following events and charting a clear course of action.

I realized that frequently it takes about the same amount of effort to pursue a dozen different courses of action. But the point really is, which one do I really want to pursue?

Usually it is difficult to name the one thing you really want most. The reason it is difficult is that so much muddled thinking hovers around the central issue that it becomes obscured. Old vague questions such as, What will others think? Would I have to work too hard? or Would I have to change my habits? clutter our minds too frequently. Clear thought comes only after muddled thought has been attacked and defeated.

External Enemies—People

We have been looking at internal enemies which must be fought if we are to live satisfactorily, at least, and happily at best. Sadly, there are also external enemies who are people who must be opposed before we can live with any degree of peace or serenity. Even sadder perhaps is the fact that we may be the enemy whom someone else must face before his life has the possibility of joy.

Opposition under these circumstances needs to be approached with love, wisdom, and restraint; but it frequently must be faced in a straightforward manner sooner or later. Tyrants still walk the land in business suits and attractive street dresses, and interfering friends and relatives are to be found nearby. Domineering spouses and even domineering children represent real threats to the happiness of the person who loves to live his own unique life—the unique life which God has given him. His only choice frequently is to fight bravely for that life or quietly give up and sink into the quicksand of oppression.

Before any attempt to oppose domination, the need for prayer is apparent. Counsel from pastors and wise friends is also a valid and needed approach.

Hiding behind the pretense that nothing is wrong, when life is being systematically destroyed, is as foolish as the attempt to hide a destructive disease. Hiding is an unrealistic answer to oppression; it only encourages more of the same.

The effective method of fighting for life against another person is seldom with angry words or accusations. Usually there have already been far too many of both, and it is probably time for a different approach.

The need for a better understanding of the situation and of yourself in the situation may be necessary for the struggle to be effective. The facts may not be as bad as you have begun to see them in your emotional state, or in fact they may be much worse, but the clear and accurate analysis by a trusted outsider frequently helps.

Basic understandings of the true nature of right and responsibilities are also necessary. There are no condemned slaves in human relationships in our culture, and if one person is demanding slave status and the other willingly accepting slavery, both have misunderstood the laws of our country and of our Bible. Freedom with responsibility is our position; unless this is clear to both parties, some real instruction is desirable.

God placed in each individual the possibilities for one life. He did not place in one body the potential for three lives and surround that one with two empty shells which had the appearance of other people. In other words, each of us has only one life to live; we do not have the authority to take the lives from others and use them solely for our selfish purposes. One life to one man or woman is God's plan. And it cannot be ignored that one life well-lived is sufficient for any person.

Sometimes the one serving in the slave position needs only to realize his true rank, which is in fact that of a free person. One of the most graphic memories I have of just such a situation occurred in our neighborhood in which a husband had arrived at the conviction that his wife was not only a constant kitchen maid but also that her logical position was to cook and prepare, scrub and polish far into the night hours. We all looked on with silent anger against the oppressive husband and mentally railed against this tyranny over his wife, who seemed to accept his domination as though it were her due.

One early autumn afternoon, several of us were sitting on our patio when the tyrannical husband looked over at his wife and said, "Honey, run over to our house and start fixing dinner. I am going to invite the neighbors over to watch the game on television and then they can stay for dinner."

My mind began to itemize the work he was asking her to do without any consideration of her plans, and I suddenly realized that she was probably already exhausted. (I had been aware of her working around her own house and yard all morning.) But before I could say, "Oh, I think that is far too much work for anyone" the situation was cared for.

She rose with great dignity and with a brilliant smile replied, "Oh, darling, I believe I had rather go take a nap." And she did.

I don't know what caused her sudden realization that she was due consideration and consultation before her time was scheduled by another person; but whatever it was, the rest of us all cheered, at least in our minds. Here had been an emancipation because someone had realized that she was no longer a slave. Her smile and simple statement were the kind of fighting for life that is hard to oppose and break down. It is very difficult to make a slave of any person who knows beyond a shadow of a doubt that he is not a slave.

Warfare is a science, and diplomacy is an art; undoubtedly our greatest victories are through the art of prayerful diplomacy. However, just as surely as there is prayerful diplomacy, there is also prayerful warfare.

God has given us the potential for such a wonderful life that we may roll out all the big guns and fire them with a cheer if the cause for which we are fighting is the right to live with joy and singing. God gave us this life; it is ours. We need not accept without struggle any human restrictions that minimize it, whether those restrictions are interior or exterior.

3

Have a Technique for Pushing Back Your Horizons by Asking, "And Then What?"

The mind is as lazy as a fireplace cat during a snowstorm if it has not been trained to resist its drowsiness. It will accept no answers, incorrect answers, and partial answers as though they were satisfying truth if it has not been prodded into more vigorous activity.

For an example of a sleepy mind dozing through an event in which it could profit from alertness, consider the very common experience of going to the doctor for diagnosis and treatment of a painful condition.

Let's say that we have gone to the doctor because of pain in the heel over a long period of time. Let's say that the pain has persisted until we are experiencing difficulty walking. After X-rays have been taken and read, the doctor gives a diagnosis of a heel spur and prescribes the use of a heel cup which can be purchased at a given health aids store. At this point we see our normal sleepy mind at work.

We have accepted the diagnosis and obeyed the instructions. We then find ourselves walking out of the health aids store with a new heel cup and no information whatever about what lies in front of us.

The sleepy mind has not inquired beyond the present moment. It has accepted the instruction for one action, that of purchasing the cup, but it has no idea of the overall picture of the problem. It did not press on to ask why the spur occurred in the first place. Is it something which needs to be guarded against in the future? How long will there be pain? How long will it be necessary to wear the cup?

These questions are certainly not difficult. They are the type of questions the mind usually experiences about any event. They are a way of saying, Tell me about this matter which is important to me.

While these are the anticipated questions, each of our sleepy minds may not think to ask them. Instead, the mind will accept a fragment of an answer and walk away. This is because the mind has not pushed back its barrier to look beyond and ask, What is the rest of the story? What happens after that? Or in other words, And then what?

And then what? is the key question in awakening the sluggish mind and pushing back personal horizons. Of course the sooner the question springs to the mind, the more conveniently it can be answered. In the case of the injured heel since we inquired no further, the doctor may well have assumed that we did not want any further information at that moment and were quite content with a hope of improvement.

But the mind which is eager to push past its own barriers and reach beyond the first answer it receives may have asked immediately, And then what?

The doctor may have responded that it was desirable for the patient to wear the heel cup for as long as six weeks before any improvement would be realized.

The sleepy mind might again accept this information without question. It now has a diagnosis and a treatment. It also has an estimated time for wearing the heel cup so it is possible that it will accept this information as the complete story. But the awakening mind might push back another barrier and ask again, And then what?

The doctor may say at this point that at the end of the six weeks there will be a fair indication of whether the heel is responding to the protection of the cup and whether the problem can be healed by the treatment.

And then what? the awakening mind will ask. What if the heel does not respond to the cup?

The doctor may say at this point that if there is no response at the end of six weeks, the future alternatives may be injections or surgery. And so the total picture of the painful heel has been sketched. The details have been supplied because the vigorous mind has pressed on and on, pushing back horizons one more step, and then one additional step.

The reason for using this particular example is that the medical problem naturally follows certain steps of development which are easy to observe. It illustrates the technique for the and-then-what? method, which is to refuse to accept partial answers as complete answers. The medical story calls to the attention that what is frequently given as an answer is, in fact, little more than a piece of the complete picture.

We have looked at the use of the and-then-what? technique in pushing back a barrier of securing a more complete answer in a conversation with another person. Perhaps more important is the and-then-what? technique applied to the thought process of our own minds. As we prod our minds into more action, we become not only the asker of and then what? but also we supply the answer to that question. We, thereby, compel ourselves to think more deeply about a question. Every hour represents situations which respond to the technique as the question forces us to look a little further, consider again, or look beyond the obvious.

Consider as an example, a conversation with yourself about the possible sale of your home. Perhaps you have been wondering vaguely for some time whether it would be wise for you to sell. Applying the and-then-what technique to the question of the very important action of selling and reorganizing your life in a new setting might run something like this:

Home Owner: I am considering selling my home because the price has inflated to the point that I can make a tidy profit.

Your Mind: And then what?

Home Owner: I will have to pay taxes on my profit.

Your Mind: And then what?

Home Owner: I know I have certain tax advantages if I reinvest in another home.

Your Mind: And then what?

Home Owner: I must find out exactly what the advantages are and also what the reinvestment time schedule is.

Your Mind: And then what?

Home Owner: Well, I will have to find somewhere else to live.

Your mind: And then what?

Home Owner: If I stay in this neighborhood, I will have to pay an equivalent inflated price for another home.

Your Mind: And then what?

Home Owner: I might wind up just trading houses and making a move without any real profit.

Your Mind: And then what?

Home Owner: I might decide to move to another area and to a smaller home which has not experienced quite so much inflation.

Your Mind: And then what?

Home Owner: This might be good because I would have less space to take care of, and if I looked carefully, maybe I could get a little garden spot also. On the other hand, it might be bad because I will have to adjust to a new area.

Your Mind: And then what?

Home Owner: I will have the expenses of a greater distance move if I do, in fact, move farther away.

Your Mind: And then what?

Home Owner: After I get into my new neighborhood, I will need to make new friends, while if I remain in my old neighborhood I will be close to my old friends.

Your Mind: And then what?

Home Owner: I will have to make definite decisions about what my priorities and real aims are. I must balance all the factors involved.

Your Mind: And then what?

Home Owner: I realize that I am down to the nitty gritty of specific emotional questions and specific financial evaluation.

Your Mind: And then what?

Home Owner: I am ready to make an appointment with a knowledgeable person to ask exact questions which must be answered by experts in real estate and financing.

Your Mind: And then what?

Home Owner: Then I must decide whether I will really be happier in a different home.

And so the questioner has been pushed to the point of decision about specific actions. The homeowner has discovered what he still must consider before he moves ahead to the point of putting a For Sale sign in the front yard or perhaps painting the entry hall and staying where he is. He has moved from the vague point of saying, "I may sell my house" to a point of specific emotional and dollars-and-cents considerations.

If he had not utilized a technique of pushing back the horizons by asking, And then what? his comfortable sleepy mind may have stopped after the first step in which he realized that the price of his house was, in fact, inflated to a number which seemed at first glance very impressive. The price might in fact seem very large after all things are considered, but the questions springing into his mind have forced him to consider all the additional information, such as tax structure, replacement cost, and costs of moving. It has also forced him to face up to possible emotional problems involved in the move, such as the need for new neighbors and friends.

This discussion is neither a plea for nor a plea against selling a house. It is, instead, a plan for a way of pushing back horizons of information until the true picture of advantages and disadvantages is faced.

We have considered the and-then-what? technique in a context of spurring our minds to get a fuller understanding in conversation with another person (the doctor) and in dealing with the solution of a personal problem (that of selling a house). Now let's consider the technique in observing our everyday life situations and the consequences of our decisions and actions.

Let's think of the little incidents which happen to each of us and to which we respond almost without thought. Therein lies the problem, we may respond without asking what the next step or inevitable result of our action may be. We may not, in fact, have learned to ask ourselves, And then what? in daily encounters.

Consider the list of situations given below to see where the events touch your days. Consider the new insights waiting as your own mind urges you to look farther.

You may say:
> I am going to call that merchant and give him a piece of my mind.

Your mind: And then what?
> (Is this, in fact, the desirable action? Do you want to ask him if you can return the merchandise rather than simply letting him know that you are angry? Would giving him "a piece of your mind" cause him to respond in anger and leave you holding your inferior merchandise? Is your genuine answer to And then what? that you have solved your problem to your satisfaction by "giving him a piece of your mind"?)

Or, again you may say:
> I am going to forget the whole problem.

Your Mind: And then what?
> (Can you actually forget this whole problem? Is this a situation which should best be forgotten, or is it in fact something which you need to solve or perhaps seek help with?)

Or you may say:

I'll buy this necessary article regardless of the price.

Your Mind: And then what?

(After you have the article, regardless of how necessary it may be, do you have a plan to pay for it? Will you have fewer problems with the article than without it?)

Or you may say:

I can't afford this necessary article regardless of how much I need it.

Your Mind: And then what?

(Can you in fact do without it? Is it absolutely necessary that you secure it regardless of the inconvenience. Can you turn somewhere else for practical and realistic help in purchasing it?)

Or you may say:

The world is getting too frightening. I am just going to stay at home where it is safe and let the world go by.

Your Mind: And then what?

(What will happen to your life if you do stay at home where it is supposedly safe? Can you withdraw and let the world go by without damage to yourself?)

Or you may say:

I refuse to spend four years studying in college.

Your Mind: And then what?

(Can you work out your career without college? What will you be doing during these four years? Does this realistically fit in with your future dreams?)

Or you may say:

I will quit my job and go into a different field of work.

Your Mind: And then what?

(Is your present job as undesirable as you seem to think? Can you work out both financial and professional details satisfactorily in a different field? Can you afford to be without a job while you are looking?)

Or you may say:

I'll get a divorce and move a thousand miles away.

Your Mind: And then what?

(Will the divorce bring happiness to you? Is it necessary to move to another area? Is this actually the action you wish to take?)

Or you may say:

I'll sell everything I own and start over.

Your Mind: And then what?

(What will you gain by starting over? Have you faced what it will cost to start over? Will you actually have anything in the new situation which you do not have in the old one?)

Or you may say:

I will cash in all my investments.

Your Mind: And then what?

(Do you have plans for a better financial arrangement? Do you have other more valid uses for your money? Will you feel good about this one year from now?)

Or you may say:

I'll join some new groups.

Your Mind: And then what?

(Do you need new friends and activities now? What can you expect specifically from these groups?)

Or you may say:

I'll settle down and spend all my evenings at home watching television.

Your Mind: And then what?

(What effect will this activity have on your mind? Will television provide a complete life for you? Is this really the life you want?)

The uses of the and-then-what? technique suggested here have been primarily applied to the adult situation, but the educational growth of children could be greatly enhanced by an application of the questioning method which is designed to push the mind on to the next question, and then to the next area.

As an example, if a child studying literature (or any other area) could teach his mind to make the next logical step rather than halting after the first facts are presented, his progress would be greatly stimulated. If he reads that certain characteristics are evident in a given period of writing and perhaps he may even laboriously memorize the names of these characteristics, he has made only the first step. The next step is, And then what?

In other words, in what pieces of writing are these characteristics found? And then what? Well, perhaps the next consideration is the question, What were the results of these characteristics being present?

For a simplified example, consider some pieces of writing of the late Middle Ages which were characterized by attacks on the system of chivalry in which feudal nobles or knights rode off from the castles to fight battles against dragons, as well as other manifestations of evil, while the serfs remained at home to work in slave-like conditions in the fields.

The student's mind may move to the next step.

Student's Mind: And then what?

Student's Answer: Great economic changes came about; literature began to attack this feudal system in satires such as *Don Quixote.*

Student's Mind: And then what?

Student's Answer: The system of chivalry began to lose its aura of glamour due to the writings, new viewpoints brought about by changing economic systems, and a general change in world conditions.

Student's Mind: And then what?

Student's Answer: The chivalric era was slowly replaced by a new era.

This progression from one thought to the next is an easy one when the mind is trained to move on beyond the barrier to the thought waiting beyond. Far too often the system of asking a question in a classroom and an answer being given has an effect of stopping the inquiring process. The student does not move on. He has answered the required question, therefore, he is finished with his work, he feels. He needs to be encouraged to move on in a steady flow of learning rather than stopping after each question or assignment as though that were some kind of satisfactory end to learning.

In effect he becomes his own teacher when he learns to ask himself the next question and to force his mind to move on. He has also learned to enjoy his work. He has rid himself of the pressure of being pushed by assignments and has begun to pace himself.

One additional fertile field for the use of the and-then-what? technique is seen in personal relationships. Here it is perhaps the most difficult to utilize since the emotion of the moment will have a tendency to drive any rational question from the mind. The system would, however, prevent many destroyed friendships, as well as family disturbances if it were used.

Consider the case of a disruptive argument among children. I use the example of children because we are accustomed to their outspoken verbal attacks. Imagine any cause or issue for their argument and then listen for the shout of anger, "If you are going to do that, you can just go home."

And then what?

If the child does go home, the result is that the angry child no longer has a playmate. Is that, in fact, what he wants?

Probably not. His shout of "you can just go home" was really only a shout of anger and not intended to be taken at face value. At that moment it was the only verbal threat which was at hand. The and-then-what? question could serve to awaken the child to this fact of confused communication before he loses his friend. If he only wants to express anger rather than play alone for an afternoon, he may be alerted to the result of his shout. This may help him change it to, "I don't like the way you are doing that; let's do it some other way." He may realize that this was his intended message rather than, "Go home."

Adult examples are just as real and perhaps more far-reaching in their results. The wife who says in anger, "Just go on without me," may need to ask herself, And then what? She may need to face up to the fact that she is excluding herself from the trip or perhaps forcing herself to come along later all alone.

"I won't do it!" always needs an inquiry of and then what? What, in fact, will happen if you do not do it—whatever "it" may be? If the results of not doing "it" are far-reaching, you may really want to say, "I am very angry about this. Why don't we talk it over?"

"I don't care what you do. You can do whatever you want to" demands a good consideration of and then what? What will be done, and will you be happy with it when it is finished? If not, the words have come out wrong. You did not mean "do whatever you want to do," but perhaps you meant, "I want to do it another way."

The question, And then what? becomes a practical brake on ill-spoken remarks, as it forces the speaker to consider the reality of his words. It is apparent that the question must become a habit, however, before its maximum effectiveness can be realized. It needs to be such a part of the thinking process that it rushes to the mind before harsh words have rushed from the mouth.

Whether the and-then-what? technique is utilized in personal conversations with others, decision making, the educational process, or as a brake on angry outbursts, it can open up new, smooth roads as it pushes back the horizons of small and large considerations. We recognize the technique as a way of saying to ourselves: There is another mental step I need to take. There is more to this matter. I need to think one more time.

Once the prodding question is incorporated into the thinking, it becomes an automatic encouragement to think again, to ask the next question, to pursue the answer which can lead to a singing experience.

4

Have a Satisfying Self-Image

If I could genuinely like only one person in the world, I would choose to like myself.

Is this an egotistical attitude? I don't think so. I think it is a reasonable position based on sound observations. Some of these observations are the following:

Until I like myself, I cannot understand what it means to like another person.

Until I see myself as a worthwhile person, I cannot believe other people are worthwhile.

Until I can believe I have a right to be respected, I cannot be at ease in a respectable community.

Until I see myself as an interesting person, I will not have the confidence to act in such a way that I will be interesting to others.

Until I see myself as worthy of affection, I cannot accept the affection of others without suspicion.

Until I see myself as an inwardly beautiful person, I cannot believe another person is capable of inward beauty.

Until I see myself as an able person, I cannot take my own or another's abilities seriously.

Until I see myself as a person loved by God, I cannot believe that God actually loves other people.

Until I can see myself as a person who has something worthwhile to contribute to other people, I cannot believe that other people can give worthwhile things to me.

Until I can see myself as lovable, I cannot accept love from or give love to others.

Until I can see myself as a rightful heir to my own space on this earth, I cannot accept another's right to his space.

Until I can see myself as capable of experiencing happiness, I cannot help another person attain happiness.

Until I see myself as trustworthy, I cannot trust another person.

These are bits and pieces of observations of a self-image portrait and its production. I speak of its "production" since any self-image produces its own aura of confidence or lack of confidence, which, in turn, produces a response of acceptance and admiration or conversely of rejection and disapproval.

If this process could be shaped into a simple equation, it would probably look something like this:

High Self-Image = Confident Behavior = Approval from Others = Higher Self-Image
Low Self-Image = Inadequate Behavior = Disapproval from Others = Lower Self-Image

The concept of a satisfying self-image may be wider than it first appears; it may extend to include an image of those near us. Recently on a Monday morning after a particularly pleasant weekend, I walked to the garage with Charles and said as he got into the car, "I love us."

We both laughed at the remark, but it stayed in our minds and later we agreed that it was a valid approach to a view of two people who are sharing their experiences, hopes, and plans for a lifetime. It was a statement which implied the following:

I appreciate and feel good about who we are together.
I appreciate who both of us are singly, as well as together.

I appreciate what you are doing in behalf of the two of us.

I appreciate the shared state of our lives.

I appreciate the portrait which our shared life paints.

While approval from other people of the portrait of lives is certainly not in itself a life goal, it must be noted that for any person to live in contentment in his own neighborhood, work in some job or profession, and come and go in the activities of his world, he needs to feel that he is a competent part of that world. His image of himself needs to be sufficiently high to give him a conviction that he is a person of some worth, of some abilities, and that he is acceptable to the people with whom he must deal.

It is interesting to note that, as indicated in the equations above, most life processes, including self-image, move in a circular fashion. The high self-image creates confident behavior, which creates approval from others, which creates a higher self-image, which creates more confident behavior and on and on the circle goes. We have only to reverse the circle to see low self-image creating greater inadequacy and greater disapproval from others can, in turn, lower self-image.

This circular motion of life extends throughout the financial, emotional, and psychological areas of life, to mention only a few. The person who is successful financially has greater opportunity for investment, which produces greater financial success, which, in turn, provides greater opportunity for investment, and so forth.

Since this is the pattern of life, it is a pattern which we should attempt to understand and utilize in our own development. As we do understand something of its nature, we realize that the small successes of every day, the small increases in our own appreciation of ourselves as God's creation, our own studied increase in the use of our abilities, are all worthwhile and important. They are a part of an ever-turning circle which raises us nearer to a level of attainment of those levels for which we were doubtlessly created.

The practical aspect of this observation is that if we can begin to build a better self-image in small areas, the image will tend to grow in the direction of greater self-confidence, which will stimulate a higher level of self-image.

This is another of those familiar areas in which the first step is the hardest and after that the progress builds on itself.

A mind-expanding question we may each ask ourselves is, What is God's ideal image of me? or in other words, How did God plan for me to develop? What was his original plan for the workings of my mind? What was his original plan for my character? How did he plan for me to present myself to the world? When you look in the mirror, does that reflection meet the specifications God had in mind? Then, after we have looked carefully at our understanding of God's view of our being, we may ask, What is my self-image? or How do I see myself? Hopefully, the images will draw closer together as a result of the consideration of the two. In the effort to reconcile the two, we may ask ourselves why we see ourselves as we do.

The complicated and involved reasons why we each evaluate ourselves well or poorly, adequately or inadequately, attractively or unattractively, doubtlessly come from every life event we have experienced. The child who was told by her mother that she was beautiful may regard herself in the mirror with pleasure for the rest of her life, even though the image which looks back at her is far from any classical or popular idea of beauty.

Why is this so? It is simply that a loving mother, in surroundings that were warm, full of trust and joy, communicated to her daughter that her particular combination of eyes, hair, and general expression were pleasant to others.

As a tiny child she saw herself as part of a world of personal beauty and total acceptance because of her appearance, and she still feels beautiful regardless of her reflection in the mirror.

Further, this personal evaluation may have been gained partially from impressions gathered from casual glances of strangers, remembered lines from stories and novels which the reader felt were applicable to him in some very real way, as well as the remarks of family members in hundreds of different situations. A feeling of beauty, gained from any of these sources unless carried to unhealthy extremes, can communicate contentment to an entire life since the person evaluates himself adequate for life situations.

The opposite side of this picture is too general and also too sad to need discussion. How many people struggle through life feeling unattractive and inadequate, utterly isolated from others, because some person in authority in their early life was harsh and unappreciative of the appearance of a defenseless child? Perhaps a child heard the word *ugly* applied to himself until he can never see himself as anything but ugly. Each of us bears a tremendous responsibility to let the little people in our lives relish the knowledge that their appearance is good, adequate, and as God created it.

But the point is that self-image goes far beyond the reality of the combination of facial characteristics and body build. Obviously, self-evaluation is based on far more than the number of acceptable and unacceptable characteristics of a face. It is, instead, made up of the emotional evaluation of how we feel we affect others. And our judgment of how they are affected may rest on highly emotional and often unrealistic memories.

These bits of memory from the past may be referred to as messages from childhood. Certainly this is exactly what they are: They are the voices which spring to our minds to say, You are beautiful because the entire family which was present at the family reunion years ago agreed that you were beautiful. Or sadly, the voice of memory may say, You are unacceptable to other people because the entire family laughed when you walked into the room when you were a small child.

If you can remember and determine what experiences caused you to evaluate yourself poorly, you are on the road to changing your self-image. You know where the problem began.

If you can see that a parent or friends assessed you as ugly or stupid in moments when they were only taking out their frustrations on you, you may be able to see how worthless and unreal their assessment was. Their assessment may be tossed aside like any other information which has been found to be false if the person can see clearly that it came from a questionable or disoriented source. Since the hurtful comment has been a part of life for so long, it may not respond readily to being tossed out of the way and may clutch and cling to the memory; therefore, help in insuring its departure is sometimes needed.

Talking the problem over with friends may help greatly in speeding the memory on its way. This is true since the remembered slights or abuses seem so much less important and significant once they are verbalized. They may even appear humorous once they are discussed openly with sympathetic listeners. It may become difficult to recall as a tragedy the long-ago, overheard remark that you were a funny-looking little thing, especially if others in the group have similar memories to compare. Such a remark, even though it has been harbored for years, can be seen as insignificant, though undesirable, once it is discussed.

Beyond the world of self-image in appearance, there is the area of self-image of abilities. It is not unusual to hear an obviously able person make such remarks as:

I can't handle that job because I can't talk with strangers.

I couldn't be his friend because I can't talk interestingly enough to hold his attention.

I can't go to parties because I can't learn to play games.

I hate open houses because I can't talk with that many different types of people.

I wouldn't fit into that group because I've never traveled anywhere.

I couldn't do that because I'm too stupid.

I can't talk with people who are better educated because they will realize how ignorant I am.

I can't write to her because she would see how poorly I express myself.

I can't talk with her because I wouldn't have anything to say to a person of her background.

I can't apply for that job because I can't meet the competition.

I can't be a member of that class because the people in there are all so brilliant.

I can't be a member of that class because I might be expected to have a meeting at my unimpressive house.

I can't go out with them because I can't return their hospitality on their level.

I can't make friends with them because they wouldn't want a friend whose family is so unimpressive.

I can't go with them because they would laugh at me.

My first reaction to each of these remarks is that it represents a terrible waste in human participation, enjoyment, and relaxed living which is brought about all because of misimpressions.

Frequently there is the misimpression of what others require of us. We feel that something difficult and precise is expected, whereas only our own personal contribution is anticipated.

Many of the statements listed here have to do with anticipated acceptance or rejection by other people. My reason for listing several remarks which seem similar is an effort to hit upon that particular statement which one of us may have as our pet remark, that one which sums up our own particular low-image response.

But here a note of common sense should be interjected to point out that no person is accepted with shouts of approval in every group in the world or should he logically expect to be. There is no reason to desire such an unrealistic situation of enthusiastic acceptance since there is neither time nor energy to participate in every activity in progress with a high level of contribution and response.

There is, in fact, something rather sad about the person who must always be the center of attention, the person who has never learned to become a part of the group and stand back to applaud others.

At best, we need only anticipate genuine approval and acceptance by our friends and beyond that we need only the relaxed right to move easily among others who do not know us well. Our need to see ourselves as acceptable does not create the need to cross barriers and expect acclaim in worlds in which we in fact could not be leaders because of the unadaptable activities in progress or the cultural group involved.

Let me give you an example because I believe this is important to the person concerned with a realistic self-image: I would not anticipate being widely accepted (and certainly not widely sought after) at a convention of oboe players. Since I neither play the oboe nor have any measurable desire to play it, I would not be the most applauded delegate at the convention. On the other hand, if I should find myself at an oboe convention, I certainly trust that I would experience a good feeling of being a listener to oboe players and, therefore, I could make a small satisfying place for myself among the audience without experiencing pangs of inadequacy or low self-image. I simply would acknowledge that I am not a leader in this situation; I am, at best, an outsider who has been permitted to attend.

I mention this instance to say that life is made up of oboe conventions or other equally unexplored worlds such as nuclear physics symposia, Stretch and Sew classes, bromeliad growing classes, or book reviews on *How to Detect Unidentified Flying Objects.* In these activities the self-image may be in jeopardy because a new world with which we individually have only a vague connection may be opened before us, and it may produce in us feelings of disorientation or at least of confusion which are destructive to the trembling self-image.

These activities, which may well be regarded as our personal oboe conventions, present an opportunity for a good experience if the person who is concerned with a problem of low self-image realizes at the outset that even participants with a self-image the height of Mount Everest need only sit back and observe the proceedings. Such a confident person knows full well that self-confidence born of a good self-image does not force outward participation beyond comfortable depths. When any of us is out of his orbit, he is not inadequate; he is simply in strange, unexplored territory; therefore, he must travel with caution.

The world is very large, and there are many activities in which we need only to relax, listen and learn, and not attempt to rise to the level of participation with excellence of conversation. Therefore, when we find ourselves in a situation where the self-image is threatened because we did not understand one word after the chairman said, "I would like to call this meeting to order," we need to relax and remember we are not inadequate, we are simply attending an oboe convention, and after all, no one needs to try to perform on the oboe unless he is prepared.

Looking back to only a few of the statements of low self-image mentioned earlier, consider the statement, I can't hold a job because I can't talk to strangers.

This problem of conversation is a threat to some people because of the misconception that they are unable to perform in some mysterious way which they think necessary to qualify, as "talking with strangers." They are unable to believe that conversation with strangers requires no performance, no choreographed response. In other words, they have built up a conviction that the task is far harder than it really is. Where the fact is that conversation requires only the ability to respond to the situation which exists at that moment, they have imagined that it is far more obscure.

This situation is, of course, not restricted to the field of conversation. If we look closely, we may discover that most activities which cause us to feel lacking may be quite simple. We have only made them appear difficult in our minds to the point of deciding in despair, I am not adequate for this task.

In most situations no grand display, either verbal or physical, is needed; only reasonable action is required. An understanding of the simplicity of the requirement builds confidence in abilities and, consequently, it elevates self-image.

True, there is a wide variation in the ease with which different people handle small talk, which is more an expression of friendliness than of sharing information. However, whether we are dealing with small talk or more serious matters, who would require that we be inspired, never-to-be-forgotten conversationalists at all times? Eric Sevareid filled that void in our civilization. We do not need to try to compete.

HAVE A SATISFYING SELF-IMAGE

All that is required to open conversation with strangers is an expression of interest which will give the stranger the opportunity to respond. These expressions may be anything from, "May I help you?" to "Did you have a good trip?" depending on the occasion. There is nothing unusual about thinking ahead of time to decide exactly what you will say in a particular situation.

Preparation in such a casual area of life is just as important as preparation in any other area. The only surprising thing is that most people assume that other people launch into brilliant, exactly right conversations each time the occasion arises. Seldom do they realize that, to a greater or lesser degree, each of us bears the same problems of relating to others conversationally.

I know a skilled man who had spent most of his early life studying and qualifying in the field of medicine. He simply had had no time for visiting, for small talk, for the small encounters which most of us take for granted. Suddenly he was involved in a medical practice where each person who entered his office needed to be put at ease and encouraged to relax before the medical questions were asked.

This was a foreign world to the doctor who had been forced to close out all such general chatter during the years of constant disciplined study. What did he do? He approached this problem just as he would have approached any other problem. With the help of his wife, he methodically made up a list of opening questions which he felt would give the patient an opportunity to respond. How is your family? Are you planning a vacation this year? Are you ready for Christmas? These are simple questions which open the door to conversation, and opening that door was the need.

The use of these questions fall into the category of a tiny skill. They represent a skill of opening a conversation;

it is a skill no bigger than a spoken word, but that is all that is required to start a conversation or a friendship. But far beyond the observation that this is a tiny skill, is the observation of the method of developing the tiny skill.

The method is the simple one of finding out what the exact problem is and then solving it. Surely a thousand problems and questions which affect our daily lives are present because we have not applied our intelligence to solving our tiny problems with tiny skills.

I have chosen only one of the remarks listed above which arise from an inadequate self-image of the ability to carry on a conversation. We have looked at a possible approach to removing this problem by concentrating on the tiny skill which can correct it. This approach of facing the problem and working out a system for dealing with it is the solution. The self-image as related to the problem can be changed as the solution is applied. We need not accept the situation as set in cement, it is not rigidly preserved for all time.

As I thought of the tiny skill necessary for talking with strangers, I was reminded of an early teaching experience. I at one time taught a course in Spanish. We had an excellent textbook, but from time to time I was struck by the impractical questions and answers the students were given to memorize in order to improve their skill in the language. Some of these questions were so stilted that they became humorous and soon the members of the class fell into the habit of greeting each other in the hall with the unrealistic inquiries which were in our text.

One such question was, "Do you know anyone whose father makes pots in Monterrey?" Obviously this question was designed by some textbook author because it included certain sentence constructions the students needed to master, but as a useful question which would ever be used in its original form, it was a bit wide of the mark.

My application is, I think that the person who feels inadequate in conversation may have abandoned the understanding that conversation is a simple exchange of whatever thought may be in the mind and has ignored the fact that seldom are we called upon to repeat some specifically structured question about making pots in Monterrey. Such stilted questions are only for textbooks.

Let's look at one of the other low self-image remarks which indicates a misunderstanding of a real situation. Consider, I can't talk with people who are better educated than I am because I'll bore them.

In friendship the operative words are *interest, sympathy,* and *relaxation.* They are not identical I.Q. or comparative degrees. You probably will not have to think more than a second to remember that one of the most popular people you know has very limited formal education.

There is sufficient general education disseminated everyday by way of television, magazines, and newspapers to satisfy any need for general conversational information. Seldom is any person in a social situation looking for a heavy input of professional discussion. The professional person has had concentrated factual conversation all day. He is looking for relaxation and contentment in social hours. This contentment is not a matter of academic brilliance but of personal friendship.

Let me tell you about my friend, Carol. Carol has a high school diploma and, as she will tell you without any embarrassment, that diploma was not from an outstanding high school, and it was not easy for her to satisfy the requirements for that certificate.

But here is the gratifying element: Carol is in demand socially with groups which bristle with every type of degree. What does Carol have that bridges educational gulfs? She has a tremendous desire to listen to good conversation, so she is the audience every talker dreams of. She has learned that it is not necessary to talk unless she has something interesting to say. She also has something greater to offer: she has herself. We who know Carol have learned from her that if we need a sympathetic, encouraging, evaluating ear, Carol is the person to seek out. She is honest but kind in her response, so she is everyone's special friend.

Compatible education is little more important than compatible eye color when each person gives what he has to give to a friendship with unrestrained joy because he has a relaxed self-image and a relaxed view of what he has to contribute.

Whatever our abilities or educational level may be, it remains that this is not a problem unless we encourage it to be a problem. We need not see ourselves as inadequate in certain circumstances; we only need to see that we have a different and unique contribution to make. If our reasonable contribution is not an oboe solo performed on a flower-strewn stage, we can be an oboe solo applauder in the audience.

A psychologist, speaking to a group of students interested in improving their self-images, recently said that one of the most destructive attitudes a person can assume is that of magnifying his own inabilities, his own foolishness, and his own little problems. As he pointed out, it is easy to magnify small oversights to the point that if there is no toothpaste in the tube that morning, the immediate response is: Wouldn't you know I would forget to buy toothpaste and have to go to work with unbrushed teeth? I will undoubtedly feel uncomfortable and drive everyone else away from me all day because they can't stand to look at my dirty teeth.

This is evidence of a poor self-image. In this person's mind so small a crisis as forgetting to buy toothpaste is catapulted into a social disaster, affecting not only the forgetful person but also everyone he contacts that day. And the reason the small event looms so large is that the person starts his reasoning by thinking: I am bound to do something disastrous today because I am a disaster of a person. I see myself as impossible so I am therefore bound to do impossible things.

This example of self-condemnation because of forgetfulness to buy toothpaste is obviously an unrealistic position, but each of us may have some equally foolish and unrealistic points of self-evaluation. These points need to be recognized as unrealistic and slowly cast aside with all our other old foolishnesses which can squeeze the singing from the life.

Below is a test to help you to determine your self-image level. Answer each question yes or no.

1. When you regard yourself in the mirror do you feel content with your reflection?
2. Do you feel that you are, in general, as adequate a person as your next-door neighbor?
3. Would you feel confident leaving a party of a group of close friends who might discuss you after you left?
4. Do you enjoy situations in which it is necessary for you to express your personal opinion?
5. Do you have good feelings remembering what you said earlier in the day when you were with a group of people?
6. When you are invited to a party, do you immediately feel that you have the proper clothing and that you will probably enjoy the occasion?
7. Do you feel that most of your friends would describe you as above average in some way?
8. Can you visualize yourself walking in relaxation through Buckingham Palace between Queen Elizabeth and Prince Charles?

Count your number of yes responses. If you have answered each question yes, your self-image level is slightly higher than Mount Everest. If you have as many as four no answers, you are probably evaluating yourself in an unrealistically low manner. Look at yourself again and start developing the tiny skills which will cause you to look at yourself with greater self-approval and, therefore, enable you to start your day singing.

5

Have a Day of Work/Treats

Any given day is two things: a time for work and a time for treats. I use the word *treats* rather than *enjoyment* since work should also be a matter of enjoyment. Therefore, the term *treats* indicates special events of enjoyment or recreation. The combination of work and treats in any given day produces more than either can produce alone. A day which rejects either work or treats is deficient, lacking in good things.

Benjamin Franklin had something to say about what he called the "little advantages" of life bringing happiness as he says in his *Autobiography:*

> Human felicity is produced not so much by great pieces of good fortune that seldom happen, as by little advantages that occur every day. Thus if you teach a poor young man to shave himself, and keep his razor in order, you may contribute more to the happiness of his life than in giving him a thousand guineas.

What Mr. Franklin said of "little advantages," I agree with in reference to "little treats." These treats can bring more happiness or "felicity" (to use his words) to our lives than the great advantages which come at rare intervals. The treats can come frequently, and they can be interspersed with work.

The concept of work (apart from the fact that for most people work is necessary) carries with it some indication of merit in most cultures. The person who works has a value. At times we may hear a cry of despair, "I feel so useless" which is simply another way of saying, "I am not producing anything," or "I have no worth as a person since I am not contributing anything of value."

A remark illustrating the value of work completely apart from the necessity of producing an income or a product was made in a conversation on a TV talk show. I do not remember who the guest was, but in response to the question, What does success mean to you? the successful speaker answered, "To me it means an opportunity to work harder."

He went on to explain that since he had had a measure of success he had been able to invest more uninterrupted time in his chosen field. He could now afford to hire others to take care of necessary but less specialized chores. Now he was able to hire assistants for research and technical help in his creative work. He was, as he said, able to work harder because of success. He appreciated the value of work itself, apart from the need for income.

By his explanation he further indicated that financial and popular success were not the complete goal of work but were, instead, a guarantee of the opportunity for further work. His remarks illustrate that work is an emotional and psychological necessity for many, to say nothing of a possibility for enjoyment.

Beyond remarks such as this one, we find a general acceptance and praise of work in most minds. General conversation usually reflects applause of work.

In spite of the general approval of work in various civilizations, in some individual minds work carries a negative connotation. Some feel that there is something inherently unpleasant in work, as though it were a burden which should be avoided if possible. Certainly too much work can tire the body and the mind and, in some cases, exhaust the spirit. But I believe that life without any work and accomplishment would be almost as undesirable as constant, hard, unrelieved work. We learn early that accomplishment carries a benediction of contentment and a conviction of the worthwhileness of life.

Where the individual does not experience any feelings of gratification from his work, perhaps it is time for him to ask, "Whose work am I doing?" Is it my own unique work which I have chosen and to which I feel God has called me, or am I filling someone else's shoes? I do, however, approach this thought with fear and trembling for a simple reason. Today the pendulum of self-understanding and self-realization through work is at the peak of its swing and is perhaps overemphasized at times. This pendulum swing is seen in those who are in financial need but are still unwilling to enter any work or profession which does not specifically fit into the category which they feel has their name on it. This is a luxury of retreat from reality. It involves blind waiting which is somewhat reminiscent of the Charles Dickens character from *David Copperfield,* Mr. Micawber (patterned after Dickens' own father) who waited endlessly though optimistically, "In case anything turned up."

Somewhere back toward the middle of the pendulum swing, however, lies that desirable world of work in which we each perform those tasks for which our talents, interests, and training prepare us.

As we work we may dream of other opportunities and accomplishments, but for any dreamer, whether his hopes are realistic or not, many practical considerations must enter. No amount of dreaming about teaching can be realized without proper teaching credentials. Just as surely the dream of being a respected businessman, cook, airline pilot, or engineer requires discipline and determination to carry out these dreams. Realization of these goals requires many steps of preparation. Happily, there is a special encouragement found in any steps we take toward our goals.

Herein enters a sometimes overlooked fact which can create contentment as we wait to enter our own unique area of work. The fact is that frustration can be avoided in the life if even small steps are consistently made in the direction of dreams. This is important because it provides a satisfying answer to the question, How can I function with satisfaction in a field which is not my chosen field? The response that even small movements in the direction of the desired field can bring contentment, is a reasonable approach to this life problem. It is an approach which makes today good while we move toward tomorrow. The alternative is to wait passively for the perfect opening to yawn before us, and for the one who waits passively, too often that perfect opportunity is slow in coming. It is good to remember that we each begin where it is possible to begin and move toward our dream as it is possible to move.

Sometimes we have false ideas about work. Years ago a young girl with whom I worked told me, with a rather embarrassed smile, that when she had earlier applied for a job with a major firm she had requested a position of executive. We chuckled at her naive approach to the world of work because we saw in her application a bit of each of our own expectations, unrealistic as they may be. As we look for and find the jobs which fulfill and enrich our lives, we would doubtlessly like to apply for the job with *Executive* in gold letters on the door, but we can seldom start at that level. Our work usually begins with a far less prestigious title.

Beginning a job and ruling out the dream of ever holding a title of honor, as well as responsibility, is to deny our own capacities as well as our dreams; however, our progress usually follows a rather predictable and patiently realized climb. This is the more usual pattern of work than beginning at the top. These dreams of lofty beginnings are usually distortions of reality.

I recall an experience, when I was in the fifth grade, which reveals another distorted view of work. I was a student in a social studies class where our teacher challenged our youthful thinking by asking us how we personally would deal with the pressure of unfinished assignments, projects, or work. With typical childish wisdom, we suggested going to the movies or reading a good story to escape the annoying pressure of unfinished work. We moved on to suggest talking our problem over with a friend and listening to the radio before our teacher interrupted us with the question, Did it ever occur to you to get the worry out of the way by finishing the assignment?

Even the class of fifth graders could see the humor of this situation. We laughed to think that we had only thought of temporary escape from assignments and work rather than the permanent escape of completing the work.

If we as adults are to wake up singing, there are probably few lessons concerning work which are more necessary than the one we fifth graders learned. The reason is, Do it! Then you can forget it! And this applies both to carefully chosen desirable work and to undesirable work which is thrust upon us by necessity.

My mother was a person strangely out of her time. She was a behavioral psychologist before behavioral psychology had been heard of by the general populace.

She made the amazing decision (and I can only think of it as amazing in view of the fact that we lived on a farm where hard work was necessary) that my sister and I should not be required to do any work; therefore, she felt, we would grow up with only good feelings about work. She felt that as a result of early freedom from work we would spend our lives enjoying it.

Whatever the chances of success her peers would have granted her, the fact is that she accomplished her goal by her perhaps questionable method; both my sister and I work far harder and longer hours than are probably necessary simply because it seems good and enjoyable to us.

These random comments on attitudes toward and experiences of work are only to say that, although our philosophies and experiences of work may vary widely, it is still generally accepted that work (totally apart from necessity) fulfills a real need in our lives. In turn work produces a contentment which is conspicuously absent when no work is accomplished.

But along with the world of work, even our own satisfying work into which we may fit like hand in glove, there is the equally desirable world of treats.

Elsewhere in this book we will look at spectacularly happy days in our lives and attempt to determine the circumstances which were present in those days. We are trying to discover the characteristics of events which brought unique happiness to those unusual days. But here, we are looking only at small treats in everyday life. We are looking at the little things which are interspersed between the jobs throughout the day. The chance or planned observations or the minute responses we experience.

The phrase *A Moveable Feast,* which actually comes from the Book of Common Prayer and refers to those holidays or feasts which do not hold to a fixed date, such as Easter, is a particularly poetic expression. Ernest Hemingway used the term as a title of his book of memoirs in which he refers to Paris as a moveable feast. The words seemed to have had a generally pleasant appeal to many writers, as shown by the number of food articles in magazines which suddenly appeared repeating the words in attractive titles.

But the Christian life much more should be a moveable feast, a continuing feast of treats. While the constant joys of the Christian life come from faith and trust, which are much deeper than the mere events of the moment, this does not rule out or in any way minimize the joy of events or the happiness of the good moments.

Life can be a succession of beautiful events if we plan
for them and stand ready to enjoy them. God has created
a world filled with everything from diamonds to autumn
leaves, from baby lambs to mountain ranges. We could
spend one lifetime just looking! Can any of us observe these
displays and doubt God's approval of our experiencing the
joy of participating in the treats of his creation?

If all of these possibilities for observing, to say nothing
of doing, creating, listening, asking, and sharing do exist,
why are we not reveling in happy discovery continually?

There are probably several reasons, but one must be that
we have not learned how to enjoy these treats. In other
words, we have not learned to dine at the moveable feast
of life or ask for service at the lavish banquet of life. We
have accepted starvation as a diet with the laden table in
front of us. Perhaps one reason for our starvation is some
misconception about our own personal relationship to God's
beautiful provisions.

One of the misconceptions may be that special treats
are for Christmas, birthdays, and Friday afternoons. Is this
a correct notion? Absolutely not. Treats are for every day
of the creative, relaxed life. Obviously the idea of limiting
joy and happiness to a few special occasions is not his idea.
Rather it is one which has been dreamed up by very limited
minds. The idea of rationing joyful events to restricted times
is a killer of happiness and the encourager of frustrations.
Every day is the day to utilize the good possibilities of
that day.

Today is the only day in which we can actually live.
We can remember yesterday; we can anticipate tomorrow;
but today is the only time for experiencing.

Another misconception, which may be tucked back so
far in the mind that we scarcely can admit its existence,
is an impression that all the little treats of life are not really
for us. Perhaps they are for the beautiful people, the wealthy

people, or the highly successful people. Perhaps there is even a haunting feeling that such pleasures and joys are really not for families such as ours. Memories of a family which worked constantly and found little time for enjoyment may create a conviction that the little joys are for other families but not for hard-working people such as ours.

It is simply another misconception that joy is not for all. The commands to rejoice, the assurance of deep peace, these come to all of us equally. Job enjoyed the feasts and joys with his family; David rejoiced with the people in the courtyard; and Jesus attended the wedding festivities, while the crowd of guests both great and small hovered around. There is simply no justification either biblically or experientially for withdrawal from the joys of living. Joys are for all of us and many of them come completely without cost. We simply need to know how to reach out to them.

There are days so hurried that there is not a moment for anything beyond work, but there are so many days which could sparkle with the addition of small special events. Such small events can change the complexion of the day if they are anticipated from the moment of awakening. I remember days which became small holidays because I bought a new book or called an old friend.

But the mind which is not accustomed to a relishing of little treats when they appear, much less pursuing little joys, may find it hard to pin down those joys which are available. A mind must be aware of what can be enjoyed before it can pursue the joy, and we quickly learn that those small experiences which bring joy to one person may not bring equal joy to another. Seldom were truer words spoken than the old adage voiced by Lucretius one hundred years before Christ when he said that what is food to one is to others bitter poison.

Since this is true, a world of discovery awaits the person

who seeks the personal joys which can light up his life, who knows that each day can include the little treats of life along with the work.

These may be little festivities which we almost stumble upon accidentally. But even beyond the accidental opportunity to enjoy the special things of today, there is the world of actually planning with care the special treat for this day. Some planning may open the door for us to:

walk through a beautiful building
invite someone over for a bowl of soup
look up a fact that is unclear
go to see a display in a downtown mall
try on a new style in a department store
memorize a poem
try a new recipe
pick up travel folders for a future trip
listen to a book review
investigate a new idea
watch a special TV program with supper on a tray
seek out a good conversationalist and have a visit
make a firm decision
join a drama group
wear well-selected clothing
pray a new prayer
send a package
make a reservation for a dinner theater this weekend
repot a plant
order a beautiful object
reorganize your address book
go to a friend's house to see a project he is working on

These are little treats? I don't know; maybe they are. Or maybe they are big treats. I have come to wonder what *big* things really are. Are they big social functions or perhaps moments of great success, or merely moments of great happiness? More and more as some dreams of my life have become reality, I have approached moments which I had anticipated as big and found them to be only a series of everyday events.

Let me cite one example. I had thought off and on through the years that the day in which I would be interviewed on a radio talk show would be a big occasion. The time came that I had three talk show recording sessions scheduled in one week. To my surprise I found myself hunting station addresses, crowding into overfilled elevators, and being ushered into rooms filled with electronic equipment, frequently with only a small stool on which to sit while I discussed books and writing with an interviewer.

The actual recording sessions were, without fail, an interesting experience. I met a number of friends in these exact surroundings, but where was the big experience? Being interviewed was but another small, good, satisfying event. There was no element of bigness in it.

I am struck by the way the memory of some small treats linger with us over a lifetime. Something small, lacking in importance, can remain at the edge of the memory like a pleasant glow. Such a glow is my memory of a bit of information which was revealed to me by a child.

I had arrived at a friend's house a little early, and June was not yet home from driving her younger child's carpool. But Joel was there to greet me. He sat on the step which the front walk made as it met the street. With his little knees pulled up under his chin, he regarded me with friendly eyes.

"Would you like to sit on the curb with me?" he asked companionably.

The idea was very appealing. It had been a while since I had sat on a curb with a small boy, who was obviously so ready to visit, so I did.

We discussed his teacher's name and what he had played today in P.E., but then Joel asked with sudden interest.

"Do you have a dog?"

"Yes," I said, my mind immediately filled with the vision of our great black beast whom we called Jeanessa. I was prepared for his next question.

"What kind is it?"

I began a discussion of the fact that she is a Collie, German Shepherd, and . . . but Joel cut me short.

"Oh, you mean she's a parts dog."

I agreed that that was a very apt description, and then Joel got a very faraway look in his eyes.

"You know," he said, "I used to think that a parts dog might have one long leg and one short leg or maybe one big ear and a little one. But Daddy told me that it didn't work out that way. And I'm glad," he added with conviction.

"I am too," I said. "I'm very glad because if Jeanessa had just one short leg with those three other long ones she would be one sad-looking animal."

And so it was because of a chance lag in my hostess' schedule that I got to have a visit with Joel and he explained to me the concept of parts dogs.

The memory of receiving this information is a very real treat.

Just recently, another friend who is a physicist with a Ph.D. told me nostalgically of a remembered little treat which was still vivid in his mind, although it had occurred when he was a child. He told me of a long-ago summer in which he spent his entire three months of vacation waiting for the mail to bring a wonderful package of balloons. He recalled that in the closing days of the school term in a rural community, he read an ad which promised a bag of rare and beautiful balloons for the price of twenty-five cents. After considerable thought, he sent off his order and

HOW TO WAKE UP SINGING

then sat back to await delivery.

Hot June days passed slowly, as the boy took his little sister by the hand and walked down the dusty road to the mailbox. As they stood together in the shade of a scrub tree waiting for the mailman, they dreamed of the arrival of the balloons.

Would this really be the day they arrived? What color would they be? What would their shape be and could there possibly be one of those long, long ones? They shivered in awe at exactly how large they would dare to inflate the delicate spheres of color without risk of a gigantic explosion.

They waited, scarcely breathing, as each day the mailman leafed through the box of mail at his side in the old car. Day after day he handed them a circular, a letter, or a penny postcard, but the package did not come.

Together the children trudged back up the road, sad and despondent, but then suddenly each day as they neared the house the same miracle happened—their sadness turned to happiness and their despondency turned to anticipation. Tomorrow, tomorrow would be the day of the balloons, they reasoned.

June became July and July became August and then one day the mailman handed them a package. Without a word the children clasped its wondrous shape and ran wildly for the house, where they fell upon it with a kitchen knife, cutting away the cords which held the brown paper. There lay the red, orange, and yellow jewels glowing in their bed of tan tissue paper.

Twenty years later he could remember the color of the oilcloth on the table where the package of balloons was opened. He could remember the number of balloons and their shapes. The day was still as real in his memory as the day it occurred. It had been an unforgettable joy for him.

I do not know why any one specific small thing is a

treat to one person and of no significance whatsoever to another. The mechanics of joy seem to defy all analysis, but the presence of these joys in all of us is seldom questioned.

There are varying joys in surroundings and occasional objects. Most people select essentially the same type of ornaments for their homes over and over because the selected type brings pleasure to them. They select the same rounded flower arrangements or the same rounded pieces of glassware or perhaps they unfailingly select slender, willowy vases and candelabra. It even becomes apparent with close observation that most people repeatedly choose paintings with the same basic horizontal, vertical, or curved lines in them. Apparently, we each feel most at ease with a particular type of line or a specific shape, as well as a definite color.

This evidence of identification with color is familiar to most of us. Colors in themselves, therefore, become treats. Women frequently move from house to house and in each new situation they recreate the same color scheme even though they have opportunity to change wall paint and redecorate with new furniture. Some people are blue people, and others are green people. Some people seek out bright colors, and others feel cornered until they are back in their own world of muted tones.

Another evidence of personal relationship and response is seen in a preference for specific arrangements of shapes. Last year at Christmas I had a group in for a buffet dinner. In the last moments before serving the dinner, a number of dishes had to be set on the buffet. A friend carried the dishes in and placed them in an irregular random pattern; no doubt they looked exactly right to her. I was close behind her, and as soon as she went back to the kitchen, I quickly changed the arrangement into a more formal geometric pattern.

In the last hurried minutes before guests were to go down the buffet line, I was busy away from the table, but I returned to find all the dishes just slightly rearranged. My friend had doubtlessly felt some compulsion to change the pattern back to the way it looked right to her.

This time I left them in her pattern, but it was difficult for me! Why? I don't know, but I felt an inner need to make the situation right, as I saw it. In this instance we were both responding to an inner urging as to what was right. We were responding to some basic shape appreciation deep in us. We each found joy in a different form. Her senses responded happily to one arrangement, mine to another.

In a slightly different, but perhaps related response area, it is possible to see the appreciation of varying shapes and arrangements extend to the point that one person finds total relaxation in a room filled with people, while another experiences a similar joy in an empty room. Here is the contrast of crowded shapes as opposed to the solitary scene which goes beyond the desire or lack of desire to be with people or alone. Further, there is the contrast of response to time blocks as seen in the joy of awakening early to be a part of the dawn, as opposed to its counterpart of the joy of sleeping late and experiencing contact with the new day in mid-morning. The advocates of either pattern of joy may find it hard to relate to the opposing point of view.

These examples and others which spring to mind lead us to appreciate the unique quality of our enjoyments. How different we all are! In each of us God seems to have placed different patterns; therefore, it seems only logical to me that there is purpose in his creative plan which is so richly varied. There must be significance in the little differences we each bear in our beings. They may be little, but they may have a potential for use and application far beyond their apparent importance.

Abraham Lincoln once said that he went to school by "littles." I discovered a new sphere of happiness by recognizing that joy is composed of "littles," even littles as small (or perhaps as great) as the arrangement of objects on a table. As my consciousness of the littles grew, I began to make a list of the small treats—events and objects which created a small rush of joy for me personally. I emphasize *personally* because the individual who wishes to wake up singing needs to look beyond the lists that others might compile for him.

Perhaps you would like to compile a list, a list of those things which you remember with pleasure. The purpose is to help you discover that pattern of response to small treats or joys which is present in you in order that you may incorporate it into your life to a greater extent.

As you build your list, you may find a pattern emerging. You may find that your small joys definitely cluster around specific places, specific forms, specific sensations, or even specific weather conditions. Complete your own list before glancing through my list which follows.

Here is a part of my collage of enjoyments or treats. They are purposely ungrouped and totally random in order to avoid any inclination to place the items in order of importance.

coffee at 3:00 P.M.
The Psalms
a fresh green salad
the theater
scrapbooks in order
an unhurried talk
trees
the opening of the church service
a fresh desk blotter
candles

a new idea
a funny statement
waking up knowing I can stay at home all day
light filtering through leaves to a sidewalk
three unread books on my bedside table
fireplaces
breakfast on the patio
high ceilings
a big roll of stamps
a small party
a freshly cleaned house
a friend seriously asking my opinion
telephone calls from our boys
tile floors
the darkness before dawn
seeing the lights come on in neighbors' houses at twilight or early morning
having friends say "I remember when we three"
the moment when guests ring the front doorbell
the ocean
the color red
antique wood
white accent pieces
library shelves
clear glass

This is a list of items which are treats. In your list you may be startled to see your responses displayed so impersonally on a page, but the listing may clarify your joys for you. As your list grows (and doubtlessly it will be different next week than it was this week), you will begin to see it as a portrait of your own moments of contentment. It makes no difference whether another person in the entire world shares your feelings, or for that matter, whether every person responds with an immediate "me too." These are personal littles, personal treats, and they need not conform to any national average.

There is a question which may come to any person who is ready to prepare his own list of joy-inspiring treats. He may say, So what if I discover the experiences of joy in my life? If I can't capture or produce them, I am no better off than if I had never bothered to think about the things which really bring me happiness.

I can only say that you may be right, especially if your list consists entirely of sirloin steak every day and emerald cut diamonds in the jewel box. However, I believe that any time we come to a clear understanding of what we really enjoy in life, we are much more likely to receive it than if we muddle along never really knowing what our goals are.

I must add also that in the most extreme cases of joy, being honestly centered in the costly, the rare, and the exotic, even these appreciations may have a purpose. Only inordinate desire for these objects becomes a problem; their appreciation may be satisfied by associations with museums rather than extensive ownership of objects of great value.

The joy of the list making for me, however, has been in the opposite direction. The identified treats have for the most part been small and readily available. They have been real and personal. Often they have been previously ignored. I have found joys awaiting when I was ready to recognize and walk toward them.

With planning, treats can be added to life daily and hourly once they have been identified. For example, the person who realizes that time spent out in the open air is special to him can consciously and consistently incorporate into his life a walk after work or at noon. Or, in a totally different area of treats, the person who discovers that straight geometric lines bring a response of rightness and rest to his mind, can satisfy that appreciation by the arrangement of hangings in his office or home.

These treats are available. They are waiting. They can be a continuing part of this experience we know as life. In them there is singing.

Honesty is necessary in making the search for our own treats if it is to have value. Without honesty no helpful steps can be taken toward the joys, for if the treats themselves are not properly identified they are further obscured.

The thought of the accessibility of joy has been the theme of much literature as in the account of the blue bird waiting in the cage at home or the man returning from the long trip to find joy on his own doorstep. There is validity in these stories since a circumstance must be viewed with eyes of joy before it can be experienced as joy. Joy is not an entity in itself. It is neither a red ribbon nor a golden box which can be handed to someone with the statement, "Here is joy." Rather, it is an attitude toward experience, toward objects, and toward events. The caged bird which suddenly appears so brightly blue gains its vivid coat in the eyes which are observing it with new perception.

When these new perceptions are developed, constant treats are available to encourage singing.

6

Learn to Accentuate the *Negative*

What? Doesn't everyone in the world know that we have
to accentuate the positive? Well, perhaps, but I believe there
is another side to this coin. There are times when we need
to take a long look at the negatives to see if they can be
transformed into affirmatives.

There seems to be some notion floating about that if
faults are just ignored, they will in fact go away. This is
particularly emphasized when there is some strength apparent elsewhere which can be brought out and admired. While
it may be a comforting thought to continuously look at
the positive, the action does suffer a bit from lack of logic.

Some of this confused logic may arise from songs which
stand as unrecognized guides in our minds without our ever
being conscious of them. We are frequently unaware that
basic thought patterns which act as standards for our important decisions stem from very little more than a remembered
fragment of song.

The song that instructs us to accentuate the positive and
latch on to the affirmative is an example of a basic thought
pattern which completely permeates our society. The affirmative philosophy is so strong that the thought of accentuating a negative strikes us as drastically wrong. However,
this very accenting of the negative at times may be the
necessary step to be taken if advancement is to become a
possibility.

The thought of looking at the positive has its charm and
its good and constructive elements since it encourages
optimism and a recognition of the joyful aspects of any

situation. Its destructiveness lies in its encouragement to ignore problems, faults, and all negative matters and, thereby, to permit them to remain untouched and unsolved. As long as the positive is regarded as the one reality, all negatives remain screened away from correction and improvement. Whole segments of our society have embraced the accentuate-the-positive point of view and have, thereby, created a situation which we might call negative blindness.

We observe friends and acquaintances charging blithely on, further developing their strengths, beauties, and recognized abilities, while they bumpily drag behind them the heavy unsightly ball and chain of one overpowering negative. This negative is some fault which is apparent to every person they meet but which is hidden from their own view by the perhaps unexamined determination to "accentuate the positive" in their own mind.

One line of the same song is totally right as it says "eliminate the negative" if in fact these instructive words mean to seek out and hunt down the defeating negative, understand the treatment, correct the fault, destroy the inadequacy, rather than ignore the negative. The tone of the song does not seem to suggest anything so serious as this diagnostic approach, however. But if we can take it to be seriously advocating the removal of the negative by concentrated effort, we are moving in the right direction.

Our need is to accentuate the negative in order to understand and remove the negative from our lives. It is time to face the negatives, the minuses, and turn them into affirmatives and pluses, not hide them behind a cover of pretense.

How real is this problem of failure to accentuate the negative in our society today? I believe it is one of the unrecognized cripplers of people both famous and obscure, recognized and unrecognized, loved and unloved, young and old.

Let me tell you of the way I was brought up short and

forced to recognize the negative, both in myself and others. Let me tell you how I came to the conviction that we must accentuate the negative.

As an adult I returned to college for an advanced degree. When I returned, I suddenly found myself surrounded by new friends and acquaintances. I welcomed the experience of visiting with my new friends. Day by day I found myself entering into their lives, even as they entered into mine.

One day I sat with eight other graduate students in a seminar room, waiting for the professor to arrive. The young woman (I will call her Joan) who was seated beside me had been strangely silent throughout the semester. She had spoken only when it was absolutely necessary to answer a question, and even then she seemed to be reluctant to share her ideas. In fact, sitting next to her as I was, I had begun to sense a constant quiet anger, an unvoiced hostility in her. She sat tensely in her chair, and her hands clasped each other rigidly on the seminar table.

Each day I exchanged a few words with her in the normal development of the course. I asked her, as I would have any other student, if she was having difficulty getting her research done for the next assigned paper. I commented on some of the material we were reading and voiced my hopes that I could work out certain rough spots before time for the final examination.

Slowly and gradually she seemed to accept me, and after a while I sensed that she was even anticipating talking with me. There was something in the way she spoke with a rush of words that made me aware that she had planned ahead to say certain things to me, to open up in conversation.

The semester moved along and we became friends, the kind of friends who wait for each other after class and walk to the snack bar to have a cup of coffee and talk over the day's class experience. We exchanged views on a dozen topics and then one day I asked her about her plans for the future. Was she going to go on for a doctorate? Was she planning to start to work? Why was she in this particular course at this particular time.

She told me that her plans were to open a public research service where she could work with corporations and individuals who were in need of intensive study on specific topics.

I considered her performance in the course which we were both taking at that time, and I could well agree that she would be excellent in providing research data. She was thorough and painstaking; her work was reliable and exact. Yes, she was indeed a potential professional researcher.

Then as our conversation proceeded she said with a burst of the anger I had observed early in the semester. "I have already tried this once, and I couldn't keep clients."

I was surprised, but since she seemed to want to talk I prodded further. "What do you mean you couldn't keep clients? Do you mean you had clients come to you but were unable to make them stay?"

"Oh, yes," she responded with considerable bitterness. "The field of research is wide open. You would be amazed at the work people want to have researched. Writers want specific areas of information to use in their writing. Salesmen want information about the background of certain products. Public speakers are always wanting illustrations and pertinent stories. Teachers want facts they can incorporate into their teaching—oh, the list is endless."

I sat rather stunned for a moment before I asked, "Well, what is the problem then? Why didn't your business succeed?"

She looked at me blankly. "I don't really know what the problem is. It just seems that the people didn't come back or didn't even want to talk to me any further about the projects after they had contacted me once."

We sat silently for awhile before she said, "That's the reason I came back to the university. I decided that there must be other things that I need to learn about research methods and systems. I just have to improve my techniques if I am going to make a go of my business."

I recalled my own early inability to talk with Joan in the seminar; I remembered her tense presence beside me week after week in the course. I compared this with the beautiful research which she had produced in her seminar papers. With considerable trepidation I asked, "Joan, do you think your problem might be a personality problem rather than a problem of competency in research?"

I was completely unprepared for the violent response I received. Joan jumped to her feet, glared down at me and almost shouted, "You're just like all the rest of them. You just want to make me feel inadequate." And with that she sailed out of the snack bar, while the students at the surrounding tables looked on with interest as I gathered my books and followed my friend out.

Joan was not in sight in the hall, so I assumed that she had either rushed to the restroom to regain control of herself or else hurried out to her car to take her bitter anger home to her apartment.

I waited wonderingly for the next class session hoping to smooth my new friend's hurt feelings, but no such action was possible. Joan sat beside me in her accustomed chair and ignored me with the coldness of an iceberg. Several class sessions passed, and I had finally written her off as an impossible case and had abandoned all intent to pursue her and win back her good will. Suddenly one day she turned to me and asked in a quiet voice. "Could we have coffee after class?"

I went happily with her to the snack bar, trying to chat

casually about the final examination and our hopes of coming out with an acceptable score. She brushed my small talk aside as she said,

"See, that's what happens every time. Eventually someone says something to me that just infuriates me and I just let them have it. That's what happened when I was trying to get my business going. Clients were always saying things that I couldn't handle. That's what ruined me."

I waited for a long while before I spoke. I had had one attack from her, and I wasn't relishing the thought of another. Finally I said, "Don't you think that some of us could help you overcome your desire to lash out at us? Don't you think that what you really need is to face and overcome your negative inability to deal with people, instead of trying to further increase your positive ability to do research?"

"I know you are right," she said. "I know I have to learn to get along with people. That is my real problem, but I just kept thinking that eventually I could become such an exceptional researcher that the personal problem of anger wouldn't matter."

We talked for a very long while as Joan finally faced the fact that she had to overcome her negative personal problem and that no amount of increasing her affirmative research skills could compensate for her inadequacy.

Fortunately this story has a happy ending. Joan accepted the fact that she had to accentuate the negative personality problem until she could get it under control. After a brief session in a therapy group, she conquered her negative. She went on to complete her degree, and she is now handling a very successful research group. She accentuated her negative until it was no longer a negative. As she said recently, "No amount of concentration on my positive ability could have brought me success. I had to bring the negative out into the forefront before I could deal with it."

My experience with Joan opened my eyes to the problem

of so many of us who go on blindly enhancing our good areas, increasing our areas of ability without ever stopping to bring those negatives out for a good hard look. There is nothing to be gained from further accentuating the positives if the negatives are still present to destroy and defeat.

But Joan's was only the first of many such examples of misplaced accentuating. Hers was only one type of negative; there were others equally destructive which began to appear all around.

Joan's problem was a personality inadequacy, but the defeating areas which we all choose to ignore as we go on hypnotized by our strengths are endless.

I was asked to serve on a neighborhood committee. At the first meeting I enjoyed meeting the people who lived all around me. As I met one after another, I suddenly encountered a beautifully groomed woman. Her hair was perfect, and her makeup flawless.

There was only one shadow on her otherwise lovely appearance. A large irregularly shaped mole at the corner of one eye caused her face to have a rather sinister appearance. The darkness of the blemish attracted attention. When I was talking with her, I frequently realized that my eyes automatically focused on the irregularity.

My neighbor and I became close friends, and we frequently visited together as we discussed landscaping and neighborhood deed restrictions. Many months passed and I became completely accustomed to her appearance, so much so that I was no longer aware of the mole near her eye. It was simply part of her general look, and I accepted it as such.

However, the day came that while we were talking, the conversation drifted to the subject of beauty appointments and personal appearance in general. I complimented her on her new hair cut and remarked that she always looked especially well groomed. In a sudden burst of confidence she said, "I've always felt that I had to concentrate on my hair and skin more than most people do. I want to emphasize my good points in order that people won't notice my problem."

I made some vague remark about our all having some problem areas, but she interrupted me with, "Of course we all have some problems, but not everyone has a terribly disfiguring mole such as I have. Why, I imagine I spend twice as much as most women on cosmetics and beauty shop appointments to keep improving my appearance just to compensate for this terrible growth." She shook her head determinedly, "I do have nice hair though, and I know that that is a real asset."

She continued to talk and again and again her words went back to the mole so after a time I asked, "Can't the mole be removed?"

She looked at me as though I had suggested amputating her right arm. "Oh, I would never do that," she said, "I have heard so many stories about problems that developed after moles were removed."

"Have you talked with your doctor about your specific case?" I asked.

"Why, no!" She said rather heatedly. "I just wouldn't have anything at all to do with surgery on a mole."

I could not let the subject drop without saying, "I am sure your doctor could tell you whether there would be any danger in the surgery. It may be that it would be a very simple procedure with no problems whatever."

We dropped the subject. As we continued to visit through the months, the topic was never mentioned again. Then, easily a year later, she arrived at my house with a smile that dazzled me as I opened the door. There she stood, the mole gone with only the slightest pink color to mark the spot where its ugly shape had been for a lifetime. She was exuberant with happiness. The disfigurement was gone.

She came in; I perked a pot of coffee and took out the best china to celebrate the occasion. She talked excitedly, "I finally admitted that no matter how much I worked on the rest of my appearance, people could not keep from looking at the mole. I pretended for years that no one would notice it if I could just develop my good points. That just isn't true. I finally had to admit that I had a problem and that I had to put all of my attention on that problem if I genuinely wanted to improve."

She discussed her first visit to her doctor and her amazement when he said that there was no problem whatsoever involved in performing the small surgical procedure. She went on to say very sensibly that if there had been any risk or any hint of possible danger that she would not have undergone the surgery, but as it was, there was no problem. She had simply finally faced the fact that she had to recognize and address herself to her negative instead of continuing to overspend on attempts to compensate with her asset of lovely hair.

Her hair is as beautiful as ever, but she is enjoying her unblemished face as well as her attractive hair. As she told me, "My attitude toward life has changed since I don't have to cringe at the thought of my eye appearing distorted by the mole."

One thing was most amazing to me, as I viewed this incident in retrospect. This woman, who was intelligent and who had enough money to have the surgery performed without undue strain, had waited so long to accomplish so simple an improvement.

I thought about this situation a great deal and eventually I had the courage to ask her about it. She admitted to a very great fear of any surgery, which may account largely for her hesitancy in talking with her doctor, but on and beyond that fear she told me of the way she had thought of her problem through the years.

She told of conversations with her mother when she was a child. She remembered her mother telling her that if she would just brush her hair fifty strokes each night, stand nice and tall, and care for her straight white teeth, no one would ever notice the flaw on her face. In other words she had been lovingly brainwashed into accentuating the positive, even as her easily correctible negative remained a problem to her year after year. She had been the victim of a faulty philosophy; she had accepted a pleasant half-truth wrapped in lulling words which had destroyed her confidence and robbed her of peace of mind for many years.

These two examples of accentuating the negative are concerned with a personality problem and an appearance problem, but many others are far more subtle.

Shakespeare is known for his creation of characters who had a fatal flaw. Hamlet had his lack of decision, and Macbeth his overpowering ambition. These flaws, which are concealed until they begin to work themselves out in the life actions, may be more similar to some of the negatives we harbor. The problem with these negatives is that we can so easily force them to masquerade as something else, something only vaguely related to the real problem.

The flaw of complaining or petulance may masquerade as an inability to endure imperfection.

The flaw of failure to be a friend may masquerade as excessive busyness.

The flaw of harshness with others may masquerade as a desire to make others perform well in their work.

The flaw of interfering in the life of others may masquerade as a desire to help.

The flaw of an unwillingness to seek out information may masquerade as a lack of educational opportunity.

The flaw of a lack of appreciation for life may masquerade as an inability to understand life relationships.

The flaw of a lack of contentment with financial circumstances may masquerade as a problem of a real shortage or lack of money.

These are negatives which need to be accentuated firmly if we are to understand and turn them into affirmatives. There is a joy in facing a problem and destroying it. There is a beauty in recognizing what must be done and doing it. There is a strength in saying, "This is my exact and specific negative, and it deserves my attention while my good positives take care of themselves for a change." As we parody the song to say, "You've got to accentuate the negative," a new cause for singing emerges.

7

Seek Out People Who Are Life-Expanders Rather than Life-Shrinkers

I heard a sermon preached by Dr. M. Douglas Harper, Jr., on the topic of "Life-Expanders and Life-Shrinkers." It helped me pinpoint and give form to a number of things which have floated around in my mind for a long time. I have borrowed his terms of *expanders* and *shrinkers*. I think they identify the situation perfectly. They say it all.

Both expanders and shrinkers are all around us, and we must admit that at times we ourselves may function in either one of the positions.

These are the words of life-expanders:

> I think you can do that.
> You will enjoy that.
> I believe in you.
> Have you seen?
> Have you read?
> Do you know?
> Let's do it.
> I'll help you.
> Try it!

These are the words of Life-Shrinkers:

> Everyone who tried that has failed.
> I don't like that.
> That isn't your type of activity.
> You'll never get that done.
> Nobody cares about that.
> Somebody will think you are trying to act superior.

Don't bother to go see that.

I don't enjoy any of that.

Just think how you will feel when you fail

After taking a look at these lists and considering their effect on our minds, I suggest that when the Life-Shrinkers close in on you, it is time to say what General Custer should have said as Sitting Bull and the Sioux warriors came pouring down to the Little Big Horn. "It's high time to get out of here!"

There just is not enough time or energy in our lives to combat shrinkers on an hour-by-hour basis, no matter how well-intentioned those persons may be. This is because shrinkers squeeze the joy from the days and make them into dry husks which suggest the words empty, exhausted, and hollow.

The spontaneous lift of spirit, the eager rush of decision, the sudden discovery of possibilities—these are not realities to the shrinker and he, therefore, cannot encourage their presence in another. The little steps toward growth which the expander notes with encouraging remarks, the shrinker views only as evidences that someone is getting out of his accustomed place.

This brings us to the question of what it is that the life-shrinker shrinks. And the answer is that he shrinks growth. Growth is his target because in general the shrinker hates the movement of growth in others. It is easier for him to keep a firm grip on another life if it is stationary; movement toward new goals and dreams too often poses a threat to the close grip of the shrinker. He cannot hold as firmly to another if that other is in a state of growth. Further, since growth tends to move in the direction of maturity, the final effect is that the shrinker refuses to permit those around him to become mature adults. Since maturity threatens to curb his authority, he feels most comfortable among those he can keep in a state of eternal insecurity.

There is a natural exhilaration in growth since it is experienced in a wide-awake situation, and it is the wide-awake exhilaration which can fall prey to the shrinker. It is difficult to believe that anyone would say, "I was so sleepy, I made great progress in my piano practice today." Or perhaps it was progress "at my job" or "at my studies."

Progress and growth are just not associated with drowsiness, instead they are experienced in the action-oriented, alert world which is encouraged by the expander and which is opposed perhaps very subtilty by the shrinker.

The shrinker, who reminds us of possibilities of failure, destroys growth potential and imposes the drowsiness of halting, insecure progress.

It is a characteristic of growth that the growing object becomes larger. The plant, tree, baby, community project, or mind grows and expands to fill a larger space. We may at times speak of something growing smaller, but this is a more specific and uncommon use of the term. In general the word speaks to us of flourishing expansion which brings a positive impression to our minds. Most of us earnestly want a growing life—a large, rich, full life. We want a life filled with good, beautiful, glowing thoughts and experiences.

Each time we read a new book, ask a question, open a conversation, look at a new item in a store, learn a new song, walk along a different sidewalk, make a trip, or buy a newspaper we are expanding our lives. We are expanding them by bringing new elements into them. We are saying: There are things out there that I want to know about. I want to explore them.

Expansion is then the end product of our growth. Growth widens the sight; the grower becomes aware of and investigates new things, new ideas, and new points of view. All of these are a part of growing life. In each surge of this growth we are either helped or hindered by our associates. We are made larger or smaller by those who stand near.

As Dr. Harper pointed out, there are both Christian expanders and Christian shrinkers, even as there are non-Christian expanders and non-Christian shrinkers.

This may seem unusual when Jesus, above all others, taught the concept of the enlarged life. He came that we "might have life, and have it more abundantly" (John 10:10). He not only enlarged the scope of now but he also enlarged the time possibilities of life. He included all of us in the possibilities of life forever, eternal life through belief in himself.

Perhaps fear or pessimism causes some Christians to feel more comfortable in shrinking their own or the lives of others; however, many other Christians help push back the boundaries of life and, thereby, become personal life-expanders. They create, by their conversation and way of life, a wider world for those around them. They enlarge the understanding of Christ and Christianity. They think and speak in larger terms and, therefore, help us all to understand something of the magnitude of Christ. In a recent Bible class during a discussion between two class members, one student suddenly said, "But don't you see that you have made God too small?"

In saying this she was encouraging all of us to see how large our God is. He is the God of all the universe, as well as the God of our own small prayer room. This person, who spoke aloud in class, was a life expander in that moment. She forced us to enlarge our view.

There was a time when Christians were generally regarded as people "who didn't do things." There are still things which Christian people do not do because of specific Bible commands, and hopefully this will always be the situation. But simple inertia, failure to move about and be aware of ideas, places, and people, has ceased to be a characteristic indicative of Christianity. We have moved to a position in which it is expected that Christians will be more aware of their universe, more apt to participate in their world because of the relationship to the Creator of that universe. Surely this is a much more reasonable attitude than the formerly restrictive position. It is an attitude of vigorous expansion based on an understanding of Jesus' teaching of abundant-life principles.

As we look back in our own lives, those people who frequently stand out as special people are the ones who in some way expanded our understanding and appreciation for life. All expanders open their eyes toward possibilities, and the good expanders open their eyes toward the possibilities of good.

On a home and family level, consider the mother who tells her child that he has the potential to be a fine craftsman or the teacher who tells the child that she has the potential to be a successful science student. These adults are expanding the lives of children toward accomplishment. They are giving children a gift of hope which is more precious than any package that can ever be put under the Christmas tree. These adults are true life expanders since they open wide the future attitudes toward life itself.

Unfortunately the actions of these helpful life-expanders are frequently offset by the words of life-shrinkers. During the past few years I have taught a number of creative writing groups. As I have talked with aspiring writers, I have again and again been confronted with stories of frustrated writing experiences. Both children and adults, with pain in their eyes, have told me stories of teachers, who said, "I don't see much in your story." "Why don't you just tear this essay up and wait until you have a better idea?" "This plot is old and worn, not worth pursuing," or even "I can't see much talent in your work." These are the words of shrinkers and their contributions are negative. A shrinker with a red pencil in hand can be as destructive as a dragon with fire leaping from his mouth.

I mention the negative presence of shrinkers in learning experiences because they need to be recognized when they come into our lives. Even the smallest child can be taught to deal with them, to recognize them simply as shrinkers who in the final analysis must be avoided as anything else which is destructive must be shunned. Most of us finally understand that even as the soothsayer said to Caesar, "Beware the ides of March" just so, we must say to ourselves, "Beware the life-shrinkers."

Along with the shrinkers of life, there are the half-shrinkers who shrink the time span of life by saying, "Not yet." Some things may not need to be done immediately, but as a steady diet the not-yet approach is little better than "not at all." The half-shrinker's message is, "Pray? Yes, but don't expect answers now. Not yet. Have faith? Yes, but expect the joy later. Not yet. Accomplish? Of course, but not too soon. Not yet." Further, they sometime distort the dream and the plan by asking, Why accomplish that when you could accomplish something else?

While wildly bending a stick across the back of every half-shrinker, I imagine each of us may remember occasions when we have been half-shrinkers under the pretentious assumption that we were wisemen or seers.

Our older son, Charles Kent, and wife, Loretta, have recently purchased a beautiful, old, rambling house in Asheville, North Carolina. I immediately fell in love with the house, and since our children are both kind by nature, they permitted me to hang things on the walls, push furniture around and do all the other things house addicts are inclined to do. At any rate, I was greatly enjoying the experience when the proud new house owners said, "We plan to strip the white paint off all the woodwork and make it natural again." At the thought of the expenditure of energy necessary to strip the woodwork of the entire house, I collapsed against the wall and hung there trembling and then Loretta added, "And we plan to strip that white finish off the fireplace and make it natural also."

Since I already had in one brief day of acquaintance come to consider that white fireplace as one of the dearest treasures of the world, only slightly exceeded by the golden legacy of Tutankhamun, I fainted and had to be revived by ice water on the face—well, maybe not quite that bad but it was almost that much of a shock to me.

When I revived I tried to suggest that they leave it as it was since there were roughly a million man-hours of labor involved in the change and, as I said, Charles and Loretta are kind; they only nodded a bit this way and that.

Not until Charles, Sr. and I were headed home and the plane was zooming over Atlanta did I have the presence of mind to say, "You know that is their fireplace, and I guess if they want to spend all that labor on it, it really isn't much of my business."

Charles, who is not famous for getting upset over such matters said, "You're right; it is theirs, and I have a feeling they will paint it purple if they want to, just as soon as you get out of sight."

As I considered the fireplace experience, I realized that I had been their half-shrinker. I had said, "Have all the fun of fixing up this fine old house, but do it my way. Work the amount that seems appropriate to me."

I don't intend to tell them that this incident is in the book until they read it. When they do, they will nod sagely and say, "That's right. It is our house." They will doubtlessly be sitting in front of their purple fireplace as they read. You see, Charles Kent is a clinical psychologist, and he knows how to deal with half-shrinkers.

Alongside and frequently overlapping the half-shrinkers are those who shrink lives with idea assassination. They may think they are helping by giving sage advice, but the effect is no less devastating than if their intent were total destruction. Too often the dream dies where the idea assassin strikes.

How often have you had what you thought was a wonderfully original idea trampled underfoot with some remark such as, "Yes, I've heard something like that before."

Two things are probably true here: First, almost no idea will be totally and entirely new. After all, is it unlikely that an idea which does not in some way grow out of some other idea and which had never before been dreamed of will suddenly come to us. But, after all, Colonel Sanders is not the first man who ever fried a chicken. He only fried it a bit differently, put it in a red striped box, and told us it was "finger lickin' good." This illustrates that it is not necessary for an idea to be totally without precedent before it has value. Sometimes only a slight twist to an old idea is quite sufficient.

Second, if an idea seems new to you, it probably has some new element in it and will, therefore, seem new and interesting to some other people.

In creative writing there is an old rule about sharing ideas before they are strong enough to stand on their own feet. Before an idea is shared, it should be so well thought out, so sturdy and sure of itself, that it can withstand even the most harsh criticism or the most lukewarm acceptance of the hearers. This lukewarm, unenthusiastic acceptance is, in fact, as dejecting as total repudiation at times. It is like someone saying, "Oh, that's OK" when we have anticipated wild shouts of approval.

The most killing thrust may come from the personal rejection, "I really don't respond to that idea myself." Such cool, if not cold, water thrown on a trembling new idea can wilt it so that it will never rise again. It is good to note that a remark such as this last one may be made by the kindest of shrinkers, but shrunk is shrunk and regardless of the inherent kindness of the shrinker, the damage is equally great once the idea lies with brown and shriveled leaves. It must be remembered at this point, however, that the shrinker bears only slightly more responsibility in this case than does the man with the idea, the one who trotted out his small feeble idea when it should have been at home wrapped in a warm blanket until it was ready to face the cruel world. The idea deserved far greater care by its owner.

I have skipped heedlessly back and forth between the expanders and the shrinkers because they, or we, are such a mixed group throughout life. One is an expander one day and a shrinker the next. I have, however, saved for the last one group of expanders to give them all recognition because I love them so. I want to send them candy and great baskets of ripened fruit—strawberries out of season. They have given me the words which say, "It is worth while! Do it! I will hold your coat." (And so frequently all any of us need is someone to hold our coats while we go into the fray.)

Some expanders have shown me roads that I didn't even know were there. Some have told me of people I might go speak to about certain opportunities. Some have even gone with me. And the difference is so tremendously great in having someone say, "Go down there, knock on that door, and tell that person that I sent you" and in having that same person take you by the arm and walk with you to that room, knock on that door and say, "This is my friend, I hope you can help her." The walkers-with can expand a hope into a reality, and they can change a tremble into a victorious charge.

How I love those people who have willingly assured me that I was able to try something even though they had no proof of my abilities. I cannot fail to thank them because they have felt no need to shape my wavering attempts into their molds.

It probably takes a great deal more courage to be a life expander than a life shrinker since by its very nature, enlargement reaches out into the unknown and shrinking pulls into itself where the old and the familiar lie. But we are on good, solid scriptural grounds as we begin to reach out toward the wider view, the new and unexplored, the beautiful and good life which lies just out of sight.

The life which lies just over the next hill belongs to God, our God, as surely as the familiar ground behind us. "The cattle upon a thousand hills" (Ps. 50:10) are his, and we are "heirs, and joint-heirs with Christ" (Rom. 8:17) to all that is his.

Therefore, we can go on growing and trying to expand without fear. We have the opportunities and possibilities for growth, and we need never surrender them, to the shrinkers' discouragement. There is too much at stake to give up the opportunity to expand daily since the expander each morning can sing a good and a rich song of growth both for himself and for those around him.

8
Have a Wardrobe That Says "Go!"

If you wake up with the question, What can I wear today?, nagging at your mind, you have awakened with a song-destroying question shading your dawn. But happily, planning your wardrobe the night before can quite effectively put the song back where it belongs.

My niece, Jean Ann Nicks, does a weekly newspaper column "Good Times" for the *Southside Times* of Tulsa. Her column is on the general art of living, and she recently made a statement about early morning actions. She said,

> The decisions which dictate the success of one's day are almost always made on an empty stomach and by a fuzzy mind. It is no wonder that people end up at work with sneakers on their feet, pin curls still in their hair, or with pajama bottoms under their skirts. From problems like these it is easy to see that getting dressed in the morning has the potential to make or break an entire day.

Empty-stomach-and-fuzzy-mind decisions are for the nonsingers, and they need to be dealt with as the defeaters they are.

Imagine this! Think of yourself waking up to a new day with a beige suit tailored to fit you perfectly hanging on a hanger at the front of your closet. Look further. Imagine beside it a beautiful silk print blouse with flects of white and emerald green on a creamy background. Now look on the chair beside your closet door. There is a new, dull brown leather bag with shoes to match. These all fit you perfectly and are just waiting for you to put them on to begin your day.

Now for the masculine counterpart. Imagine waking up to dress in your new gray jacket and navy pants. Picture the navy and white patterned tie with just a fleck of red draped over the palest blue shirt. Then look at the softly shined shoes with matching socks. Look on your dresser where your wallet and pocket secretary lie waiting for the day.

How would you react? Just what would be your attitude as you get out of bed and began to dress? How eager would you be to start your day?

Now contrast this with another picture. Think of yourself waking up, glancing around the room to see a pile of soiled clothing in one corner, and a closet door ajar, revealing a disorderly jumble. Visualize yourself straggling over to try to select clothes for the day. See yourself pulling out one wrinkled blouse or shirt only to stuff it back into the closet because there is neither shirt nor pants to coordinate with it. Imagine yourself taking out crumpled dresses and jackets, realizing that this one has a spot on it and the other needs to have the hem adjusted from some long-ago mini length.

What a beginning for a day!

The point is obvious. But more important is the question: Why not permit ourselves to awaken each morning in the situation first described? Why not provide ourselves with the relaxation and joy of awakening to the possibility of entering a day with style and even real beauty?

I have described a situation in which new and possibly costly clothing hang ready for wearing, but the newness is not necessary for creating a daily wardrobe which can bring a song to every morning. "New" is not the operative word. "Costly" is not the operative word. *Satisfying* is the operative word.

It is absolutely necessary that we have clothing that we

are content with. We need to feel that our clothing is suitable and right. But far beyond the minimum of basic satisfaction, there is the possible added satisfaction of feeling that we look just great, that we look as well as we personally can look, that we have utilized every possibility within us for beauty.

Does this seem like a dream to you? It shouldn't. It is a reasonable goal for any person who is willing to put in the time to accomplish the goal. But how do you do it?

If you had to conquer a history course in order to qualify for a high school diploma, what would you do? You would study history until you had mastered the required work, wouldn't you? Exactly the same technique is necessary for mastering the clothing competency test. We all must study clothing until we have mastered the field. We will still make errors in the daily tests of putting outfits together, but few people ever arrive at a point of 100 percent competence in any field, so we need to be ready to settle for a nice high score somewhere short of perfection.

The reason mastery of clothing is so important is simply that once it is mastered, it is out of the way and off the mind. We are at ease once it is cared for. We have to pass the history test only once. Although we have to dress each day, an understanding of the clothing field is required only once. After that it is a matter of recalling and constantly reorganizing the information we have gained. We add new facts to our knowledge each season, but basically we utilize again and again the same facts, thoughts, and evaluations we have gained and stored away.

The question of where to go to study clothing is a real one, and I think the best answer is that the first place should be a long study session with your own full-length mirror, a treasure which every person should own even if it is the most inexpensive model the variety store has in stock. The second place for study should be with an admired friend who seems to know how to dress well, in other words, someone whose style in clothing you would like to copy. This should also be a person who is inclined to build up your confidence in yourself rather than tear it down. Confidence is important because a part of successful clothing choice comes from a relaxed discovery of what the wearer's very best self is and how he can reveal or demonstrate the best self through appearance.

If in your first conversation with your well-dressed friend you discover that this person is simply not a communicator, a teacher, or a confidence builder, move on to a new teacher. This is very important since many people who have difficulty with clothing constantly look back to some discouraging experience which destroyed their interest and enthusiasm.

A friend of mine attended a course offered by a highly reputable department store. This course was widely advertised as an opportunity to learn what clothing would enhance the learner's appearance and create new confidence and beauty. The course failed in both respects for my friend. The information was not applicable to her situation, and the suggestions were not explained in such a way that they could be utilized on a day-to-day basis. The course simply was not for her, and it became a memory of her one futile excursion into the world of fashion and personal development.

I believe the fault was more that of my friend than the department store, however. She could have written the experience off as an unproductive one and moved on to another teacher in a different situation. If this same friend had eaten in a highly advertised restaurant and found the food not to her liking, she would not have abandoned interest in food; she would simply have gone on to a different restaurant next time. Perhaps we are too timid and vulnerable in seeking help with our appearance. We take our instruction too seriously. Maybe it is time to look at the whole field of help as a cafeteria of instruction where we may select what is applicable and interesting and move on without either anger or annoyance to the next serving table which serves our needs better.

Keep in mind the general plan of looking at our friends and any available personal instruction which we may study and then accept or reject without either feelings of defeat or anger. Let's go back to the first part of our plan, that self-help session in front of a full-length mirror.

As you stand looking into your mirror, do you have a realistic mental picture of how you want to look? As you stare into the mirror, can you visualize how that person staring back at you would ideally appear? If you do, you are already on the road to being successful in clothing planning. If you do not, answer the following five questions and see if you can arrive at a picture of the direction in which you wish to move.

1. What general type are you: frilly, fancy, tailored, outdoors, business, or casual?
2. Can you recall a single outfit you wore to any event which made you feel completely self-confident? Visualize yourself again in that outfit.
3. Can you decide exactly what it was about that outfit that made you feel so confident? Was it the drape of the material? Was it the style of the skirt? Was it that it had long sleeves, or short sleeves? Was it the type of neckline? Was it the color of your shirt? the pattern of the tie? the fit of the pants?
4. Do you believe it is possible for you to look attractive on every occasion?
5. Are you willing to take the clothing situation sufficiently serious to achieve the highest possible attractiveness?

If your immediate reaction to the first question is "I am the _____ (select your own) type but I am too dumpy, tall, short legged, long legged, frail, big boned" or whatever, my only response is *ridiculous!* The day of any limitations because of a given body type is long since gone. You have only to think for a moment to recall someone who is just your type who is recognized as a real beauty in our society. This is as it should be! Sad, indeed, and limited is any society which can only recognize the beauty of a single type. The only point for consideration is, What type of clothing will enhance the beauty of my individual type? This is the area of reality! The world of "if I were . . ." is pure masochism and should be shunned as completely as the plague.

Perhaps your answer to the first question is that you are a combination of the several types, or you may be a clear-cut casual type, for example. Perhaps you can visualize yourself only in sports clothes. Wonderful, what could be better and what could be more in tune with our cultural pattern. But each of the other types is equally fortunate.

Any limitations we feel because of type, exists only in our own minds. Inadequacies because of natural characteristics are dark bugaboos which need to be recognized as pure foolishness and quickly chased from the mind. Each of us can be equally attractive and even beautiful. As you study yourself in the mirror remember this statement, Elegance comes in all shapes. The word *elegant* means tastefully fine, and neither the Mona Lisa nor Pinky has a monopoly on tasteful fineness.

We can each recognize our type and deal with it elegantly; this is our aim.

Let me suggest a little exercise which will enable you to appreciate your own particular size, shape, and unique combination of features. Get a scrapbook and begin to fill it with attractive pictures of people who share your particular characteristics. If your face is long and narrow, cut out the magazine and newspaper pictures of handsome faces of women or men who have your particular facial structure. Cut out the pictures of attractive people who have your particular build, your long or short legs, your long or short body. Study the clothing these people are wearing, study their hairdos and their posture. Study them as figures in a textbook of beauty.

As you develop your scrapbook, you are doing far more than simply accumulating pictures and making a collection of photographs; you are learning to evaluate beauty as it exists in your own individual, unique case. You are learning to appreciate these characteristics which God has given you. Further, you are learning how to enhance the gift you have been given.

I would particularly suggest this scrapbook exercise for any young person who is grappling with the problems of growing up and is finding it hard to accept his own being in the body which he finds himself. One young man may identify his own long-armed, long-legged body with that of the basketball players who are adding scores on the court. The young lady may see her own body shape as that of the lovely models displaying the first beautiful fashions of spring or fall. A short boy may realize that many prominent men are inches shorter than he had realized. A young girl could discover that special clothing is being designed just for people of her type. All of these have begun to discover their place in the world. It is a little hard to feel insecure when you realize your dimensions are exactly those of Mary Tyler Moore, or to feel slighted when you discover that your face is, in fact, shaped exactly like that of Princess Grace or, for that matter, Prince Charles.

Now return to reevaluate your answer to question 1, the question of your general type. Now consider whether the analysis of your style type is really true. Have you simply drifted into being a tailored type because it seemed easier to dress in that way? Is there a being down within you shouting for a white silk shirt with hand painted cuff links? Or on the other hand, did your mother and your friends overencourage you into a silk shirt with ruffled cuffs when you actually wanted to wear a bright, striped blazer with a turtleneck sweater? Only you can answer these questions. But ask yourself seriously, Am I a peacock dressed in little brown hen feathers? or Are these peacock feathers suffocating me while I belong with the stately brown hens marching by in simple understated simplicity? Again, only you can answer those questions. They are both part of the first question, What type am I? It is a critical question. It deserves a well-considered answer.

Questions 2 and 3 ask us to remember some outfit in which we felt completely at ease. This is an invigorating and challenging exercise! Try to recall the length of the skirt, the fit of the jacket, the cut of the shoulders. What was it that made you feel so good as you wore that outfit? As the answer to that question dawns, store the details away in your mind for future reference, not once but each time you purchase or sew a piece of clothing. Plan to duplicate them again and again in other jackets, dresses, skirts, coats, pants, or shirts.

As I face this question, I think of my white suit. I visualize the length of the jacket and realize that the midhip-length jacket is good only because of the cut of the skirt. I cannot wear the jacket with pants, it is too short for the pant look, but is right to balance a street-length skirt. I like the sleeves that are amply long since I have long arms and have to be very careful in buying jackets and blouses. I think of the scarf I wear with the blouse, and I realize that the neckline would be too stark with small jewelry or an open collar shirt.

And so it goes. As we analyze the costume that looks

best on us, we need to hold fast to the analysis for we are choosing the lines and shapes which enhance our bodies.

I believe that anyone who can achieve the look that really pleases her one time, has opened the door to achieving that look everyday of her life. The problem is in the first time, the first achievement. As we work on it, set the mold, and arrive at the understanding of that first good experience, a pattern will fall into place. In other words, if a yellow turtleneck with a gray tweed skirt made winter dressing a pleasure, consider a gray summer skirt with similar lines and a yellow printed blouse for summer. Don't waste your research! You had a winner last winter, repeat that winner with slight changes this spring.

Do you really believe that you can look attractive each day? question 4 asks. This is a question of motivation and of personal assessment. If you honestly answer no, then ask yourself, Why not? If you simply do not see yourself as an attractive person day in and day out, consider the reasons for this self-evaluation. Did someone tell you that you were unattractive, or have you just not as yet discovered your own potential? The poster saying "God don't make no junk" is a part of our times, and I am equally convinced as I look around that "God don't make no uglies." We create the ugly parts of our appearance by failing to utilize and treat with respect the characteristics God gave us.

The last question concerns our willingness to take our appearance seriously and to work at elevating it to a high level. This is, indeed, our own personal challenge. This task is neither the easiest nor the hardest in the world, but it is probably one of the most rewarding. It is a matter of personal decision.

Let me tell you about a friend of mine. Marcia (not her real name) is a tall angular girl with flaming red hair. When I met her, she dressed with utter disregard for her appearance. One would have assumed that she had no interest in how she looked. As we became good friends, it suddenly became obvious that she did care very much about her appearance; she simply had decided that it was impossible for her to look attractive. She had tried to ignore the entire subject. This decision to ignore is a very difficult and unrealistic one to follow since it is necessary for every person to deal with clothing hourly and daily. Let's face it! It is the law of our land that we dress in something each time we leave the house. Nudity is looked on with little favor!

Marcia would probably agree with this fact; it was her decision, conscious or unconscious, to hide her own appearance behind a wall of carelessness. She once confided in me that she would not wear any scarves or jewelry because she was afraid people would think it was funny that such an ugly girl was trying to look pretty.

This is a sad, distorted view. However, this attitude, in varying degrees, is probably expressed by many people. In Marcia's case a number of circumstances, including a new job which required her to look well-dressed, caused her to face up to the clothing and self-care situation. She faced it with imagination and verve when it was necessary. Now she is not only attractive but also strikingly handsome, as she has learned to accent her vivid coloring and dramatic build. She looks like a bright page from a full-color style magazine. I believe Marcia is one more example of someone beginning to realize her true potential. Growth is joy! Happiness is an expanding horizon!

As we think of clothing, the topic of money rears its ugly head. There is an inclination to think that money can solve all the problems of appearance and wardrobe. It is true that an unlimited expense account would make clothing selection and purchase easier; it is just as true that money alone cannot guarantee beauty. If you doubt this statement, take off an hour and walk through the aisles of your city's most elegant and fabulous department store. Observe the people buying beautiful and costly pieces of clothing. Look again! Are they all beautifully dressed people? Look again! Amazingly, you will discover that the general appearance is very little better than that in a much less costly store. Why is this so? It is simply that money is not the magic answer to attractiveness; knowledge and careful selection are the answers. There are dozens of ugly dresses and ill-designed, difficult-to-wear dresses hanging on the racks of the finest store. Money is not the talisman when it comes to clothing. Good old know-how added to a modest budget will achieve much more than indiscriminate spending with little or no planning and observation.

Observe, learn, then purchase, these are the good steps toward singing in the mornings while you get dressed for the day.

Edith Head, the clothing designer who has created clothing for the movie heroines since the heyday of dramatic costumes on the screen, stated that anyone could learn to look glamorous. She described the many starlets who came to her offices appearing drab and uninteresting and who went away appearing attractive and even beautiful after her skillful hands had created the ideal wardrobe for them.

While our aim may not be glamour of the movie variety, still Miss Head's statement about the possibility of increased attractiveness by careful clothing selection is an encouragement in a real sense.

Someone has said that the really contented person is that person who is able to appear externally as he feels he is internally. I think this statement is true since it indicates the wholeness of being able to present ourselves to others as we really are. There is a barrier erected between people when they are unable to communicate to each other their true natures. Though this barrier will undoubtedly be overcome and removed if people are together for awhile, still it is pleasant to know that you appear to be a successful businessman, an interesting interviewer, a responsible parent, or any of a hundred other categories which you fill.

Only once have I been a victim of mistaken identity, and I can recall this event minutely since it was not only frustrating but actually frightening. I never again want to appear to be someone I am not.

We had the very dubious pleasure of boarding a riding horse in a small stable behind our home. Although I had grown up on a farm and knew at least a little about horses, my city-bred family harbored some deep conviction that a horse was much like a pet dog that would immediately feel at home with us and happily trot up when he heard a familiar whistle. Charles and the boys were convinced that Rusty would stand around like Trigger just waiting for Roy Rogers to appear. As a result of this impression, they were rather unconcerned about fastening the gate and tethering the horse since they were sure he would never leave us. Eventually the anticipated occurred, and we awoke to find the horse gone.

Since the boys were in school and Charles was at work, it fell my sorry lot to try to find the horse. I advertised in the newspapers, called every horse association I could find listed, and tramped through every undeveloped acre in the area in the vain hope of finding the horse. Eventually I began to get responses to my newspaper advertisements. One call was from a woman who described the horse in detail and told me exactly where he could be found.

The intermittent rain did not deter me as I went several miles to the wooded area where my caller had told me a horse was roaming loose. The woods were near a house, but a road ran past the property and on into the woods.

With empty halter in hand, I plunged into the woods, whistling and shouting. I covered the area and then started back for the car halter in hand when I was suddenly surrounded by people with very threatening looks on their faces.

It seemed that there had been a number of horses stolen from the area and these proud horse owners were in far from a sympathetic mood toward a stranger, halter in hand, walking through the area where their horses roamed. Just visualize yourself standing in the rain with an empty halter in your hand, trying to convince irate horsemen that you are not a horse thief or even an intended horse thief. Well, that's the way I felt. I showed my driver's license and other identification, which of course impressed no one since obviously a horse thief was as likely to have a driver's license and credit cards as anyone else. Eventually they became convinced that I was at least a very poor thief since I was doing my work in broad daylight with a car and horse trailer parked on the road for all passersby to see.

In those moments, I knew what it is to appear to be something which I was not. This feeling is doubtlessly shared in different situations by hundreds of people everyday. An intelligent, beautifully trained person may appear to be very ordinary; a sensitive, interesting person may appear to be rough and unconcerned. The facts from the inside may not have as yet communicated themselves to the outer self.

So there is reality to the clothing situation. It is one more item in the dictionary of terms of life experience. It is important since it has a definite effect on other aspects of life. Singing is just easier, and even automatic, when we feel that we look as well as we can and look like that person whom we know is living inside us.

9

Learn How to Keep the Continuing Delights Going

If we keep something going, we do it continuously and regularly. It becomes a thread or a connecting cord lacing our days together. We have spoken elsewhere of treats, or isolated good experiences, but here we are thinking of continuous, recurring delights which are practiced over and over.

I have become convinced that the most contented and joyful people I know are those who have learned the art of holding their days together by *continuing delights*. Often these delights are so small and secret that they are unnoticed by others. Over a period of time, they may become almost unnoticed by the person enjoying them.

Other continuing delights are large and life shaping and are often instantly observable by others. But far beyond the importance of attempting to classify the delights by size or even by the level of enjoyment they produce, there remains the fact that such continuing delights can be present in our lives.

Last night I talked by phone with our son, Charles Kent, who told me that four inches of snow had fallen during the day in Asheville, North Carolina. Immediately I had a mental picture of his and Loretta's home perched like a hesitating bird on the side of a mountain.

"Did you manage to get home in the car?" I asked.

He told me that the car was parked at the foot of the mountain and that he had walked home. I groaned loudly, but before my groan was complete, he interrupted me, "Oh, it was just a ten-minute walk in the fresh snow. And," he added, "there's nothing in the world like the first snow-fall."

I could hear the delight spilling through his words. He had had the pleasure of a ten-minute walk through the first beautiful snowfall of winter. It's beauty and quietness had permeated his being. That's what I mean by a delight. It was a delight which still clung to him like a benediction, although he had been home for an hour or so.

A first snowfall comes only once a year, but it is only one evidence of the continuing delight of the changing face of the seasons. There is some aspect of that face which can be enjoyed everyday. We may need to encourage ourselves to see those aspects. They are there, waiting to be relished.

One day at a meeting of Authors Unltd. of Houston, the group of ten members suddenly got to talking about "a place of rest." The place of rest we were talking about was a place of mental rest where we could each withdraw frequently and find peace waiting for us. In a matter of a few seconds, a number of people described in detail the place to which they directed their mind when the pressures became too great or sleep would not come at night.

Guida spoke of walking down a long path between trees, and Gloria described, with the accuracy of frequent observation, a place beside a lake where the water lapped against the shore and lulled her to sleep. Ida and I admitted that we usually mentally journeyed back to the farms where we had grown up, hers in South Texas and mine in Oklahoma, but then I realized that my place of rest had expanded. In addition to journeying back to the trees and rocks of the hillside, I was traveling more and more back to the faces of those I loved and also to a well-remembered list of those people who in my life have said to me, "I love you." It is a good place to rest.

Returns to these places of rest are some of the continuing

delights of life. The concept of a place of rest is certainly far from new; it is only revisited each generation and by each individual. The Psalm 91 tells with beautiful detail of a place of rest where we may "abide under the shadow of the Almighty" and say "He is my refuge and my fortress." Millions of people know this biblical secluded place, and they have gone there so frequently that their minds immediately visualize the waiting path and the open door to serenity. "Rest in the Lord," Psalm 37:7 tells us. "Rest" and find the continuous delight of knowing your strength is renewed for the hours ahead.

The withdrawal in the mind to rest and relax in contentment may be a small action, but the result of the withdrawal can change the general tone of a life. And so it is with each of the continuing delights which can be a part of the passing days if the life admits the opportunities to discover them.

I like the word *ambience* which means the environment or those things which surround us. When I think of the places of rest, I think of them as places which provide a mental ambience of quietness. I want an ambience of peace for my mind and heart in order to find, in my outward world, a greater ambience of continuing joy. I believe this is a realistic goal. God's Word says it is possible.

Let me tell you about another continuing delight of an entirely different nature, which was introduced to me by a woman who does not remember her advice. In fact, she did not attach any importance to it when she gave it to me. It has meant much to me because it convinced me of the importance of going to see everything that's moving. When I first heard this advice, there was always much work to be done at home, and there was usually some question in my mind about whether I should take the time for little excursions away from home.

I had worked the first few years of our married life, and

it was only after the birth of our first baby that I was at home all day. This baby was a lovely little person who could scream louder and resist more strongly than most people three times his age. He had plans of his own from birth and working a schedule around him was much like working a schedule around the wind. I threatened to give up all activities and stay securely at home, dealing with the baby and his schedule every moment. It simply seemed easier than struggling with him. Then a very wise neighbor told me, without the least emotion, that her children had all been vigorous self-planners, and she had solved the problem by taking them to see everything that was moving. "It gave them something to think about," she said.

"Go to see everything in the city," she told me matter of factly. "Take him with you and if he doesn't like it, go see something else." Then she added, "Of course you know this is what we all need to do for our own education, go see everything that's moving."

We went!

Our next-door neighbor later told me that our baby was the only true outdoorsman in the neighborhood. I wrapped him up in blankets and toured every house being built in the adjoining subdivision. Together we talked to builders, examined floor plans, and observed trees being taken down. Soon the baby was a little boy, and on we went. By this time we had widened our territory until we took in all zoos, junk stores, museums, wrecked houses, and new shopping centers. We watched men laying pipe for drainage and women illustrating how to sew with zig-zag stitches. Together we discovered one of the continuing delights of life; we discovered the continuing joy of going to see everything that's moving.

Recently a friend said to me, "I never sit down without a piece of needlepoint in my hand." She was participating in one of the continuing delights. Another friend said, "I keep an active file of recipes I want to try. I plan toward the moment I can test them." She was enjoying another continuing delight. I have a brother-in-law who is a ham radio operator. This is his continuing delight.

I think that reading is one of the most wonderful continuing delights most people can ever experience. For those of us addicted to this delight, we would no more get caught without a good book than we would get caught without a key to the backdoor. I used to get weary on long weeks in a tent when the masculine three-fourths of my family fell in love with camping, but later I became the most avid camper around. I could sit in a camp chair and read from first light until it was too dark to see or until an unwary park ranger walked up and startled me out of the world of Dostoyevsky and sent me into wild steady screaming while he was standing there in full uniform saying, "Lady, I'm a Ranger. Lady, I'm a Ranger." But that's a different story.

Music is a continuing delight for millions; it is the kind of joy that adds another dimension to a busy day or waits in the jacket of a new record until that special moment when the listener can sit down and absorb the sound without interruption. It knows no one season for appreciation; it overflows each month and week and remains from the earliest breakfast hour when the radio is turned on very low in the kitchen, to avoid waking those who can afford to catch a few more winks, to the last sound in the house at night. It is a continuing delight no larger than a sound; it is as effective a force as the mind can contain.

There are also the delights of tiny events which are repeated and repeated again within a family. The marshmallows cooked in the fireplace on cold nights, the picnics to celebrate a July birthday, little trips, little occasions recurring on schedule among family and friends, but sometimes these have to be thought of, planned for, and scheduled.

Sometimes we are very slow to observe such possibilities for a continuing joy.

For years our family had clung like well-trained monkeys to the high stools at our kitchen bar. This perch had seemed convenient for a growing family in which each member needed to run out the door at any moment. It was easier to hand a bacon and egg plate to a child on a nearby stool than to set a table with napkins and silver. Quite suddenly I realized that the number of eager hands reaching for plates had diminished. Only Charles and I were present for breakfast, and there was really no rush. We are early risers and we had plenty of time so why not move into the dining room? We now sit in splendor in the dining room and drink coffee from china cups. And do you know, it doesn't cost a cent more than it did to hang on the stools in the kitchen. I'm amazed. It is now one of our continuing delights to breakfast in the dining room where we can look out the windows, across the patio, and watch the seasons change.

Then there is the continuing delight of consciously developing vigor. Vigor is active strength or force. It is physical or mental energy or power. It is vitality and intensity and the development of each of these characteristics is a life-changing delight.

I have discovered that there are certain questions which come to my mind to help clarify my enjoyment of the delight of development of vigor. These questions frequently come at the close of the day and help me prepare for a more vigorous tomorrow.

In questions far less structured and formal than they are stated here I ask myself:

> Do you actually feel excited about tomorrow?
> Do you have one specific pleasant plan for tomorrow?
> Do you have one goal you plan to achieve this month?
> Have you broken this large goal down to include a
>   single small goal for tomorrow?

Do you feel that you absolutely must get up in the morning?

If I answer yes to each of these questions I feel that my approach to that day is a vigorous one.

I have spoken elsewhere of the circular motion of life forces and nowhere is it more apparent than in the area of vigor. The life which is characterized by movement, enthusiasm, concentration and verve becomes steadily more able to utilize enthusiasm, concentration, and on and on. And so the life of the person enjoying these activities becomes daily more vigorous. On the other hand the life which is characterized by lack of movement, pessimism, distraction, and inaction becomes more and more lacking in power and force which in turn encourages more lack of movement both physical and mental. So it continues like a globe turning on its axis and never escaping the circular pattern.

I was interested to discover that one of the characteristics of depression is the physical tendency to sit down and remain in one place. The body of the person in deep depression seems to be unable to respond to normal inclinations to get up and move around. The desire to sit down in a miserable tight heap is overpowering and very real. As we can easily see, this state of lack of stimulation from outside forces brings on even greater depression. This picture only emphasizes again that inaction encourages greater inaction even as vigor encourages greater vigor.

But although we agree readily on these evidences of depression or conversely of vigor, we realize that at times we find it difficult to discover specific steps which lead toward vigor. We want to ask, Where are the handles to clutch on for a climb toward the continuing delight of pursuing vigor?

My answer is, Ask everyone you know. I say ask everyone because the first person you ask, even though that person may be a very vigorous individual, may give you a poor answer. That person may live a vigorous life, but he may not have analyzed the situation of his own life and reduced it to words. There is no need for discouragement if one person gives you a poor answer. Move on to the next person and ask the same question. This questioning is vigorous action in itself. It is a vigorous pursuit of information, and you can pursue an answer until you are satisfied and convinced that you have found your own satisfying response to the problem of vigor.

Your answer may lie in discovering compelling interests which will activate your days. It may lie in discovering ways to use a talent fully. It may lie in facing a problem and removing it so you will be free to operate without despair. It may lie in finding ways to participate in stimulating activities which are real to you. And here lies a clue to the nature of vigor. True vigor must be based on reality— real interests, real accomplishments.

Let me illustrate what I mean. Tomelane Gaskamp works with horses. She teaches riding and has compiled a textbook, detailing each movement of the rider while in the saddle, as well as a complete program of care for the horse. Vigor literally radiates from Tomelane when she tells of her work with her riding students and the horses. Horses are real to her. She believes in horses. She finds goodness and stimulation in being around horses, and vigor grows from the reality of her interest.

She illustrates the dictionary meaning of the word *real* in reference to her interest as it states that the word means "true; not merely ostensibly; being an actual thing; genuine." This definition conveys the depth of the thought of the word. The thing which is real is significant and of great value. It is sufficiently worthwhile to move one to action.

So the question is, What is real to you? When each of us discovers what exists with stark reality for us personally, we will have tapped a source of vigor.

Pens and sketch pads are real to Kimball. Every white, empty page is an invitation for him to cover it with lines and shadows.

Drama is real to Olivia. Each long-remembered speech is a separate jewel to her.

Sailing is real to Don. Monday morning finds him with firm plans for next Saturday's sail.

Poetry and prose portraits are real to Susan and Julia. They pursue them with creative intensity.

Art is real to Dortha. She is a gallery guide at a museum of fine arts and sparkles at each painting she can show and grieves over each painting she must pass by because of lack of time.

Cooking is real to Annette. She goes to the home of foreign students on the Oklahoma State Campus to learn to cook dishes from other countries.

Antiques are real to Helen. She studies every new book on the subject, climbs through attics, and lugs suitcases all over Europe in pursuit of treasured objects.

This list could go on and on, but the point of the listing is twofold: First, to point out that each of these people derives vigor from a real interest. They would be different people without the interests. They would be pale representations of themselves without their vigorous interest; second, to point out that the energizing interests vary widely and are highly personal.

In order to discover what is real to us, it may be necessary to lay aside coverings of superficial concerns. The magic is found in throwing off these artificial layers of concealment to find what is near and valid to our own being. If it is bird watching or hot air balloons, that is what it is. The interest will probably remain present in some form throughout the life whether we permit ourselves to express and enjoy it.

Let me suggest an exercise to help you look into yourself

to discover the interests which qualify as real.

The following is a checklist of seventy-five possible interests in widely differing fields. (The list could of course run into the hundreds or even thousands.) Do not read through the list casually, rather look carefully at each item to determine your level of interest in that specific area. Then rate each interest as to a five-star interest, four-star interest, three-star interest, two-star interest, or one-star interest. Reserve the five stars for those interests which put a sparkle in your eye and which cause you to breathe a bit more deeply just thinking of them. Reserve one star for those which you can take or leave alone.

When the chart is complete consider it as a whole. See where the four- and five-star areas fall. Are they mostly concerned with people, homes, events, sports, skills, academic areas, or crafts? When you discover that general area which is most real to you, you will be ready to say, I have a real interest in the general area of _____. I have a continuing delight in it. Then look at those interests which you have awarded five stars. These are the areas of specific real interests, which when pursued will bring excitement and vigor to your life.

Circle the number of stars which indicate the level of interest which you feel.

travel	*	*	*	*	*
science	*	*	*	*	*
magazines	*	*	*	*	*
rearing children	*	*	*	*	*
money	*	*	*	*	*
keeping in contact with friends	*	*	*	*	*
machinery	*	*	*	*	*
tennis	*	*	*	*	*
letter writing	*	*	*	*	*
refinishing furniture	*	*	*	*	*

boats * * * * *

cooking * * * * *

philosophy * * * * *

sketching * * * * *

automobile * * * * *

sewing * * * * *

Bible class * * * * *

exercise * * * * *

gardening * * * * *

lecture on the topic of your choice * * * * *

thinking * * * * *

history * * * * *

ballet * * * * *

clothes design * * * * *

teaching * * * * *

home decorating * * * * *

swimming * * * * *

music * * * * *

gourmet specialties * * * * *

football * * * * *

prayer * * * * *

oil painting * * * * *

hanging baskets * * * * *

golf * * * * *

psychology * * * * *

baking bread * * * * *

building houses * * * * *

hiking * * * * *

horses * * * * *

china * * * * *

sex * * * * *

bird watching * * * * *

trees * * * * *

collections * * * * *

table games * * * * *

poetry   *   *   *   *   *
dinner parties   *   *   *   *   *
choir work   *   *   *   *   *
committee work   *   *   *   *   *
reading   *   *   *   *   *
dogs   *   *   *   *   *
books   *   *   *   *   *
art objects   *   *   *   *   *
Christmas decorations   *   *   *   *   *
calisthenics   *   *   *   *   *
conversation   *   *   *   *   *
housework   *   *   *   *   *
records   *   *   *   *   *
dolls   *   *   *   *   *
bicycle riding   *   *   *   *   *
house painting   *   *   *   *   *
fishing   *   *   *   *   *
glass   *   *   *   *   *
flower arranging   *   *   *   *   *
hospital procedures   *   *   *   *   *
needlework   *   *   *   *   *
telephone conversations   *   *   *   *   *
cats   *   *   *   *   *
words   *   *   *   *   *
zoos   *   *   *   *   *
pianos   *   *   *   *   *
jewels   *   *   *   *   *
efficiency studies   *   *   *   *   *
beauty aids   *   *   *   *   *
weaving   *   *   *   *   *
social service   *   *   *   *   *

If we could see the stars each of us have circled, we would know a great deal about who we are and how we would enjoy passing our time. As we evaluate our own charts, we can begin to discover what our real interests are and in turn find what will bring vigor and singing to our lives.

Another continuing delight which is practiced on many levels, varying from intellectual discussion to over-the-fence chatter, is the delight of conversation. This delight requires only a willingness to listen to others and to observe and think to the extent that we have something with which to respond. I personally feel that good conversation (and probably every person would define *good* differently in this context) is among the most civilized and civilizing of man's activities.

There are no rigid requirements for conversation. It is apparent that conversation with one person or one group will be totally satisfying, whereas a totally different experience the next day will be equally satisfying. In other words, it is a flexible experience. Herein is the joy.

When my children were babies, Lamoss Moore was my next-door neighbor. We sat and talked together for many hours (I imagine we would both blush with embarrassment if we knew how many hours) as I cradled a fretful baby on my lap or helped an eager three-year-old learn to tie a shoelace.

Lamoss and I had conversation!

We talked earnestly in low voices; we talked seriously in determined voices; and at least once we shouted violently in loud voices and were bitter enemies for ten minutes, after I flounced angrily home and stood wringing my hands, until she showed up at my front door and shouted in a mock operatic voice, "Do I have a friend in this house?"

We had good conversation, and the memory of it brings happiness to me now. We still get together from time to time; when we see each other, we pick up where we left off the last time, with no break. We have the continuing delight of conversation (I almost wrote shared conversation, but I believe the important thing is that conversation by definition must be shared, and doubtlessly that is a part of the reason for its pleasure. It is a sharing of minds and of thoughts and the more original and helpful that sharing is, the more enjoyable it will be.)

Conversation is not only the exchange of ideas, but it is also the puns or quips or even just little remarks which are indications of a state of mind, even these can be remembered aspects of some good talks. I have stored in my mind remarks picked up here and there in scattered conversations over the years. They are bits and pieces of the life of a specific remembered day as it was capsulized in words.

For example, around our neighborhood I heard: "My husband keeps suggesting that I wear my black dress. Frankly, I think that he is trying to tell me that I'm getting fat again."

A good conversation with my small son yielded up, "I'll put the toys in my-tility room." What could be more reasonable? I had been telling him for months, "Put your toys in the *u*-tility room."

Beverly came in huffing and then stated dogmatically, "The trouble in our family is simply that I am a long-range runner married to a short-term sprinter."

Our own nine-year-old, in the midst of what I thought was an illuminating geographical conversation about our neighbors to the north, carefully studied a picture and then asked, "Mother, what kind of a horn is this beatnik playing?" Sure enough, it was a Canadian glass blower complete with cap and long tube with a bulb of hot glass at the end.

Our own highly indignant grocery store checker had this snappy conversation to pass on as her customer admitted once again that he was not a savings stamp collector. She said, "If you had taken all the stamps I've offered to you in the past year, you would already have a thermos bottle and be going for a Cadillac."

There is always a rangy son who stands up from the table after a less than exciting meal and in his best conversational tone says, "Mother, this is a nice place to visit, but I wouldn't want to live here."

Who can forget Lynn Burke, our pastor's wife in Mandeville, Louisiana, who concluded a conversation with, "When I was a child, they said I was bullheaded; now they say I am determined."

And husband Charles passes on this bit of sensible wisdom, "If you're timid, don't try to play the glockenspiel."

Then there are the bits of wisdom which filter through and remain a part of our permanent thinking, such as the casual remark that everyone on the block fusses about the clutter; then we stop and think that most of the clutter we complain about is the clutter of abundance. The closet wouldn't be cluttered if it contained only one dress, neither would the pantry be cluttered if it held only one bag of rice.

The wisest gal on the street recently said, "After fifteen years of marriage, I can say with conviction that whether the verdict is win, lose, or draw if it is in a bitter fight with your spouse, you both always lose."

And I am looking forward to long conversations with Thoreau. I would like to spend perhaps an eon talking with a man who said, "Morning brings back the heroic ages"; however, I face the fact that getting an appointment for conversation may be a bit difficult with a man who says, "I have a great deal of company in my house; especially in the morning, when nobody calls" (from *Walden*).

And any man who observes that "none is so poor he need sit on a pumpkin" and also considers picking huckleberries for a living has some interesting slants on life, especially if you are inclined to pumpkin sitting or huckleberry picking.

I have saved for the last continuing delight the delight

which runs through our lives day by day like a burnished silk tie connecting one good day to another, and one peaceful night to the next. It is prayer.

Prayer is sometimes hard work; it is frequently much easier to plunge on headlong than it is to stop and talk with God. But in spite of this difficulty, the delight of current prayer experience ties life's events together to form a pattern.

Nina once told me that as she awakened each morning she prayed first for her family and then for those people in the cars she could hear roaring past her apartment home. This is a continuing delight which has become a part of her schedule.

Wonderful experiences through prayer are logically to be anticipated, not stumbled upon in amazement. While it is true that we experience amazement as we meet God face to face in prayer, it is the amazement of wonder at its joy and not surprise that the encounter has occurred.

Paul spoke of the "peace of God that passes all understanding" (Phil. 4:7). This term, this combination of words, has become a part of our body of Christian understanding. It has become a goal and gift to be desired.

The expression, "The peace of God that passes all understanding," is a combination of words which exactly expresses the idea. Where most terms only hint at the reality of an emotion, these words recapture it. No person, who has ever known this peace even for a moment, can question the meaning of these words. It is the peace which is so satisfying that it cannot be understood by the human mind; it does in fact pass beyond our understanding.

It has been my experience that these intervals of perfect peace may or may not be connected with significant events. This seems noteworthy because it is so incredible that God would grant such a blessing of contentment in unremarkable times of normal living when no special prayers are being offered for great strains or decisions and only the daily events of life are passing in review. An experience of the "peace of God which passes all understanding" came to me recently on a morning of normal activity.

I was working to complete the manuscript of this book. I had talked with my editor earlier, and he had expressed approval of the title, chapter titles, and general tenor of the book. I had set Christmas as my deadline for completion of the book. I have learned what many others before me have learned: Unless I set a deadline for finishing, a book may stretch on and on into years of writing.

The normal Christmas pressures were beginning to build as I pressed on through chapters 9 and 10. I was greatly enjoying the work, and I felt good about the progress of the book. But the nagging worries of the busy season were beginning to tell on me.

There was a party that night and my dress needed hemming. I had a cheese spread to prepare for the party and a few phone calls to make about general Christmas details. Then over all of this, there was the need for total concentration on the manuscript.

As I sat down at my desk early in the morning to begin work, my mind was as disorganized as a flock of wild birds flying. I picked up my Bible for a brief reading and then bowed my head for a prayer. A friend in the Bible class which I teach on Tuesday mornings had told me that she wanted to discuss some Scriptures we had touched on lightly in class, and her face sprang into my mind as I prayed. She had frequently mentioned that she was unable to be confident of God's close presence in her life. As she came to mind I prayed for her.

I asked God to give her confidence toward him and then I found myself praying, "And let her know how natural and good it is to live with you and to understand how you give peace to make every day contented."

As I prayed, an answering voice came to my mind, Why don't you pray this for yourself? I sat back almost gasping as I realized that of course, that was what I needed more than anything else for this particular day when I was pushing so hard for accomplishment.

This mental question was followed by a rush of peace which was both mental and physical. I felt a relaxation and a complete trust in the personal care of God and the goodness of the day. For the first time I knew there was time to write the chapter, hem the dress, make the cheese spread, and deal with the telephone calls. I suddenly realized that only I was tense about the events; God was not tense. He is complete and utterly beyond tension and pressure, and he is in control of the situation and perfectly able to add peace where he wishes.

The peace that passed all understanding was mine in that moment, and it remained throughout the morning. I cared for the business of the day, but I moved in a different world from the world I had known earlier. God had given me his peace; I had experienced answered prayer about matters of which I had not had the wisdom to pray. He had implanted in my mind the understanding that he is a God who does not experience stress. I had lived a good lifetime in the brief moments of one prayer experience.

The significance of the realization that God is not tense is important because of its implied results:

> If God is not tense, he will never deal with us in irritation.
> If God is not tense, he will never deal with us in frustration.
> If God is not tense, he will never deal with us in undue hurry.

From experiencing the first snowfall of winter to praying the prayer which is answered with a peace which will be remembered—these are as one. They are the continuing delights of life. They await only our determination to keep them flowing consistently and richly in our lives for the joy of the song.

10
Learn How to Yell Creatively for Help

The word *creative* means "original" in its strictest sense; however, in popular usage it has been expanded to include the thought of unrestricted, free, joyous, and arising from a source of the individual being. It is the free and unrestricted aspect of the word creative which applies here. The creative screamer (or yeller or crier or hollerer) is the one who has mastered the art of crying out for help from his own free, honest and unlimited heart.

We usually think of screams or yells as loud, piercing shrieks or cries, but there are also those little barely audible cries which are just as surely a plea for help. The impact of the barely audible cry can at times be greater than that of the screeching outcry, and the response can be equally helpful. And surely the quiet cry for help may be far more acceptable to the hearer than the loud, strident shout. Like many other things, screaming is an art and a science. Whether we have admitted it or not, it is a part of every life at some point.

The wise and well-oriented heart screams for help when it can no longer carry its burden alone. It screams with vigor and with anticipation of an answer. When the answer comes, it shouts thank you for all the world to hear. This is good screaming! It has a reason and a purpose; when the screaming is over, the screamer is not only relieved but he has also grown stronger by the good exercise of wise, shared vocalizing.

Screaming for help is vastly different from whining because screaming anticipates a solution and an improvement.

Whining merely comments unpleasantly on the circumstances. The following is an example of whining. Several years ago we were selling our home. I greatly enjoyed the activity since we were anticipating a new home. As I showed people through the house day after day with the inane remarks such as, "And this is the bedroom," I found real enjoyment in talking with the prospective buyers.

One day after an earnest money contract had already been signed on the house, a woman came by and asked to see the house just in case the other sale fell through. I showed her around, and she told me again and again how much she liked the house. Then she looked at the kitchen and said, "This room is certainly far from an ideal kitchen."

I mumbled that we liked it, and she continued, "I just don't like a kitchen like this at all; in fact, I couldn't cook in an arrangement like this."

I finally laughed and said, "Well, you won't ever have to cook in this particular kitchen because the house is already sold."

My visitor was not deterred for a moment as she answered, "I just can't understand why you put a kitchen like that in this house."

I have thought of this incident many times during the years because it is such a classic example of whining about circumstances which are of no concern or pertinence to an individual. I suppose the reason it struck me as being so classic an example is that it typifies the irrational aspect of whining when the whiner does not anticipate any result whatever coming from the unpleasant recital of impressions. My visitor was not asking me to change the kitchen; the kitchen bore no personal relationship to her; still she spent energy recounting the problems as she saw them.

This example of whining about situations never need be confused with creative screaming, which is a clear-cut plea for help, a distinct shout for assistance, or a lucid call for relief.

Some people have difficulty learning to scream. They have been taught that only weak people scream, that no one responds to screamers, that others do not respect a screamer, and in general that screamers are an unattractive lot. These are misconceptions. Screaming can be pleasant and surrounded with dignity if the screamer has learned the rules of creative screaming.

Screams for help come from that part of our beings which admit that we are not all-sufficient, that there are times when we must turn to others. It is an act of humility and recognition of the reality of our frailty and how frail and vulnerable we are!

The stiff, stern self-dependency which caused generations to turn from cries for help with disgust may have created a pioneering people, however, it also sealed off the possibility of living in a community of man with relaxation. The thought that a man might be "beholden" to another if he accepted anything from him created isolated people who lived and died without ever experiencing the life outside their own minds. There are people who still feel this way. They are unable to share life. Self-discipline and personal strength are two of the most beautiful characteristics to which man is heir, but they can be carried to ridiculous ends of artificial and unreal existence.

The story of one Victorian author's mother is told to students to illustrate the spirit of unrelenting self-discipline which was applauded in that era. It is said that after a tour of Europe in a horse-drawn vehicle, she reported with pride that never once in the entire journey did she permit herself to lean back in the carriage.

I believe this traveler would have profited from some instruction in creative screaming—screaming for a pillow to rest her back, as well as shouting for release from the strict convention which encouraged her to sit unyieldingly mile after mile and day after day. I am inclined to wonder if she ever laughed on the trip. I do not know. But it seems a bit difficult to equate enjoyment with the stiff-backed posture she brings to mind. Excessive rigidity both physical and mental has undoubtedly caused unnecessary discomfort, loneliness and fear as well as deprivation of real necessities.

When we do embrace the concept of screaming for help, we all face the challenge of learning to scream both effectively and pleasantly. We also face the challenge of learning when to scream and, more importantly, to whom we should scream.

Let's look at the last part first. To whom would we scream? The answer is to scream to the person who is capable of giving wise help.

One year when our boys were around nine and twelve years of age, we went on a wonderful vacation to Padre Island. We camped on the beach, cooked gourmet chicken and broccoli in a pressure pan over a fire of driftwood, and swam in the warm gulf waters, which that weekend were the clearest I have ever seen on the gulf coast. Along with the unusually clear water, there was also an element of flukiness in the wind and tides. (We learned later that the great fish and sharks from the deep waters unaccountably came in close to shore.)

In the afternoon the boys and I went out to play in the surf and in the calm sunny afternoon we were each lying floating about lazily on an air mattress. Suddenly without warning a gentle swell picked up my mattress and carried me out from the beach. I am a fair swimmer and have always felt completely at ease in the water so I rode on the swell looking back at the boys who had gotten off their mattresses and were regarding my ride with amazement.

I rode out, expecting momentarily to find the swell releasing me and then carrying me back. This did not happen, and suddenly I felt real fear. The boys were disappearing in the distance, and I clung to the mattress and rode on out. I told myself that the waves always returned to the shore. I told myself that any minute the water would rush back, and then I opened my mouth and started to shout to the boys, "Help me get back."

With a terrible shudder I realized that I must not shout for them to help me. They could easily come out and be drowned so instead I managed to shout, "Go back. Go back." They stood like little statues for a moment, then looking over their shoulders toward me, they turned and started back to the sandy beach.

Then after a moment, very gently, the water lifted me and a wave carried me back and deposited me in the shallow water.

The point of the story is this: It is unwise to scream for help to people who cannot help you or who would possibly be harmed by trying to help you. The accomplished screamer must learn this lesson early. Don't scream to small children in the shallow water; shout to the man standing on the deck of his yacht with Coast Guard approved life preservers in his hands. And (but you are already ahead of me) not incidentally that One standing with the mammoth life preservers in hand is frequently, usually, if not always, the same one who can reverse the billows, control the tides, direct the winds, and shape the clouds.

God tells us to scream to him when we are in trouble and when we have problems. In his wisdom he is in no danger of rushing out into water over his head. "Call upon me in the day of trouble: I will deliver thee" (Ps. 50:15) is his instruction for our desperate scream. To me this is one of the shortest and most beautiful messages I have from God. This is the message of one who knows how to deal with my screams and my life as well as the screams and life of everyone who calls to him.

What we are talking about are the cries of our prayer life, but there are others, in addition to God, to whom we may scream. Their responses may be less perfect, less complete, and less understanding; but the fact remains that those people with whom we share the forms and contours of our lives are also available to answer our cries.

Often we are too proud, too confused, or too timid to cry to others, but God is clear in his instruction about the reltionship of his people. We share our lives to some degree, as a result of our sharing the same days and the same world. We share time and space. But our relationship goes deeper than this. We are told, to cite only one example, to "do good unto all men" (Gal. 6:10), and implicit in this thought is the sharing of troubles—the doing of good to others when they need help.

This month I had the principle of sharing troubles with friends illustrated for me in an unforgettable experience. This is Jean Brown's story, and the name has not been changed to protect her identity for Jean's story is a story of victory through answered prayer and answered cries. It is a story of crying out and being heard both by God and by many friends.

Jean called me just before Thanksgiving with a sob in her voice and a half apology for "bothering" me. She said that she had to talk with someone about her problem. She had not slept for several nights, and she was worried to the point of desperation.

Jean's problem was that she simply did not have enough money to live on.

She had been divorced for a number of years after a long marriage. She had an eleven-year-old son, and she received only token child support from her son's father. Earlier, she had come to Houston to build a new life and had managed to find a fairly good job as an accountant with a travel agency. Before long, however, she was asked to change her hours to work late in the evening, a situation which was impossible for her since her son came home from school early and there was no one to care for him if she was away.

She took another job with a considerably lower salary but with a promise that she would receive a raise in pay in six months. She and her son, Jerry, simplified their lives to make use of every available cent of income and braced themselves for six months of austerity. They shopped carefully for food; they cut out all entertainment expenses; they agreed to do without any new clothing, and they counted the money for school activities with a careful eye. Their one big shared event before the change in job had been a little dinner at a restaurant each week, but that small celebration also had to be abandoned.

Six months passed and events worsened. Jean received the word that in spite of earlier promises, there were to be no raises at the company where she was working. She also received the word that her apartment rent was to be raised at the first of the year.

This was when Jean screamed.

As we talked, she told me that about a year ago she had decided to tithe her income. She said that she wanted to continue this practice regardless, that she felt that God wanted her to do it even if she could not at the moment see her way clear to making expenses. She told me with great faith that God would take care of her and Jerry even if she could not see how God was going to do it.

I asked her if she minded if I told some other people of her problem, and she said without embarrassment that her need was far too great to try to hide it behind any pride. Her child's future was at stake, and she was without any new resources. Then, with her eyes full of tears she said what millions of parents have said throughout the years, "But how can I tell my child that there will be no Christmas this year?"

That night, with Jean's assurance that I could discuss her problem, I called a number of people in our Bible class and asked if they would like to help with Jean's Christmas. Roberta, our unofficial class secretary, helped me call and then helped me keep track of the money as it came in.

Every person we called thanked us for being asked—or in other words they thanked us for passing on Jean's scream for help. After a few days we delivered an envelope of money to Jean and explained that her cries about a Christmas for her child had been heard.

The first week in December passed, and Jean talked with me several times about the possibility of looking for another job, but she felt hesitant about making another change since it often looked unstable to have a job record that reflected many employment changes. Near the middle of the month, however, she attended a Christmas party and talked with a friend who told her of a job opening with a major firm. Rather half-heartedly she began to prepare a resumé to submit with her application.

About this time she was called to her home in Mississippi because of a family illness. When she returned, she called me and her words put the Christmas spirit into my season.

Her Christmas mail had been waiting for her with a letter in a bright pink envelope with an unsigned note in untraceable printing in it. Along with the note was some money, just enough to cover the expenses of her unexpected trip home. We ended our phone call and shortly afterward our pastor arrived with an envelope of money that someone had asked him to deliver anonymously. After his visit Jean again called me with an exultant note in her voice as she said, "How could all of these wonderful people do this for me?" Then as we were talking, her son came to her with the day's mail delivery in his hand. On top was a Mailgram from the company where she had just applied for a job.

I waited as she read the message first to herself and then aloud. It was a request for her to get in contact with the personnel department to schedule an interview.

In jubilant voice Jean said, "We just asked God to take care of me. We didn't have any idea he would do all of this."

"All of this" was the result of honest, open, vigorous screams, first to God and then to friends.

Those of us who had a small part in Jean's scream received something almost as great as she received. We were permitted to see God at work. This principle is very important. God is at work constantly, but sometimes we may miss the evidence of his lifting and carrying. Another result was that we were permitted to help with the work, and regardless of the age or the circumstances there will always remain a joy and a peace when we are able to help another person.

When we were living in New Orleans, I knew an elderly lady who spent her days visiting and encouraging other elderly people. Once when someone commented on her work, she said that it was the thing that gave meaning to her life and that it was a constant pleasure.

The person talking with her then remarked, "But I'll bet that if anything ever happened to you, you won't let anyone help you because you are so able and independent."

To her surprise the woman answered, "No, you couldn't be more wrong. If I ever need help, I certainly won't deprive others of the joy of helping me."

To me, this was a surprisingly perceptive view of an old thought. We are quick to admit that there is great joy in helping others, but we are more restrained in permitting others to help us. There is a reality and lack of pride in the statement that we do good for others when we permit them to help us. This has been largely covered up in our modern way of thought. For many of us our way of thought may need to be reconsidered where the screams for help are concerned. But the screams themselves also need to be looked at.

Fortunately for all of us, our screams to God can be very casual, unstructured, and unconsidered. The words may be poorly chosen and the thoughts may be jumbled, yet God understands. But with human friends the situation changes. Before screaming to a friend it is wise not only to know what we are screaming about, but also what we are screaming for.

This may seem obvious, but it is not always easy. If I scream that I am cold, I just might receive a coat. Maybe what I really need is a wood-burning stove since there is no other fuel available for my home. I may have a number of coats in the closet. Therefore, my scream that I am cold may be very confusing to another human, regardless of how eager that person is to help me. Both the stove and the coat fight the cold, but they are scarcely synonymous. It is hard to warm a room with a coat, and it is hard to wear a stove.

Most needs may be more complicated than this, but the principle remains. It is the responsibility of the screamer to scream intelligently. This principle is particularly obvious in the child who may scream and resort to whining because he does not like school. In reality his problem may be that he needs help in preparing a classroom project which is worrying him. The cry, "I hate school," is a general scream, while "please help me with my science project" is a specific and even a sophisticated scream. It requires an analysis of the general frustration to realize that the science project is the specific issue involved.

Unfortunately, this matter of confused screams is not

restricted to children. Adults are likely to scream for help with their general depression when they are actually frustrated by an inability to communicate with their spouse on a particular subject. Just as likely, adults may scream in general about a lack of opportunity for personal development when in reality their problem is as specific as an inability to make a decision about which course to enroll in at the local community college.

Problems seem to have a built-in potential for snowing us. They usually appear broad and far-reaching at first glance, whereas they become more specific when they are studied further.

Life hands us specifics. They cannot be dealt with as generalities. "I need a ride to work" (a specific), often is voiced as "nobody ever invites me to ride with them" (general). "I want someone to go with me to the movie" (a specific), may become the general "I don't have a friend in the world." "I can't decide on a good menu and recipes for a buffet" (a specific), may be stated as "I am the poorest hostess in the world" (general).

This difference between the specific and general is important for the creative screamer. The reason it is important is that the specific problem can be communicated to another person and, therefore, solved; whereas the general problem is little more than a rush of unidentified emotion which is almost impossible to deal with.

In approaching friends with our cries, therefore, discretion and sophistication need to be exercised. This discretion is not necessary just in order to avoid exhausting others (although this is a thoughtful consideration at times). Our need for sophistication in shaping distinct cries is for the purpose of receiving the answers for which the cries were voiced.

Looking through the haze to discover the real problem

before we scream leads us to the need for selective screaming. We need to separate the genuine need from the imagi-
nary and the important from the trivial. Or perhaps we
may need to cry to a friend for help in discovering whether
the problem, indeed, is important or trivial.

It is fortunate, we may well notice again, that God requires no such selective screaming. Instead, he urges us to
bring all problems to him whether we understand any part
of that problem.

However, there is a value in selective screaming even
in our cries to God, and it is this: As we scream selectively,
we force ourselves to think more clearly and analyze more
exactly the shape and color of our problem. As we do this
careful analysis, we automatically force our minds to deal
more realistically with our concern and, thereby, become
more open to sound and rational help in making decisions.
God does not require us to clarify our problems for his
convenience. He has no problems of confusion, but the
process of clarifying the problem brings understanding to
us.

Seldom are our friends so skilled in help and counseling
techniques that they can pinpoint our exact problem if we
do not give them an accurate picture when we scream. We
have probably heard of the helpful person who poured
water on his drowning friend to revive him. Many of us
have received our share of reviving water simply because
we did not make ourselves clear when we asked for help.
Let me suggest as a working principle that the screamer
is responsible for the clarity of his scream. While this may
be true, however, it remains that each of us also bear the
responsibility for attempting to understand another's cries
for help.

Here are five questions to help you determine whether
you are a creative screamer or whether you need to improve
your screaming technique before vocalizing.

1. Do you pick the person to whom you scream because of his wisdom and discretion rather than because he is a close friend?
2. Before you scream do you make it a habit to distinguish between a real problem and an annoying situation which will pass?
3. Are you usually able to cut through the haze of emotional detail surrounding the problem to determine the real issue?
4. Do you usually know exactly what result you wish to gain by screaming for help?
5. Before screaming, do you prepare yourself by making a conscious effort to put your problem into exact words which describe the situation clearly and accurately?

If you answer yes to at least four of the five questions above, you are well on your way to being a creative screamer.

11
Rediscover the Art of Play

Does *play* sound like a word from a different world than your own? When you hear the word do you feel a bit annoyed that an adult would be so childish as to consider play as a reality? I imagine this is true of many people, but I have come to look at play as a very real part of life, perhaps even a necessary part of the relaxed life.

From observation, I feel that play may relax and even heal minds and bodies which are subject to constant tension and strain. It may provide some helpful experience of return to an earlier rested state as a rubber band returns to its original form after the tension of stretching is removed.

The present return to walking and jogging seem to affect both muscular and mental tone, and certainly these are forms of adult play. It cannot be denied, however, that some adults are able to rob these activities of their enjoyment aspect by making a job or task of them. The tense jogger, who is exercising only because his doctor has recommended the activity, may jog with gritted teeth as he mumbles, "Only ten more minutes, and I will be through." In this case the element of play is removed.

On the other hand we have all heard confirmed walkers and joggers say, "My exercise clears my mind of worries, and I feel fit all day." From these two examples we see that there is something more to play than just the movement of the body; there is also an attitude of play.

For a glimpse at the play attitude, stop to remember the times when you were a child playing in the yard. Remember running as hard and as fast as you could, shouting to other children, breathing so hard that your whole body moved with your great gasps for air. Remember how you felt mentally, remember how there was not any thought in your mind except winning the race or shouting some wonderfully silly word to your friend who was running beside you.

That was play!

How long has it been since you had that feeling of complete relaxation?

The *Random House Unabridged Dictionary* lists some seventy-four definitions of the elusive word *play,* and most of the definitions have something to do with action and also with doing things without any serious intent. "Without any serious intent!" What a wonderful thought! How we need some of this mix of lack of seriousness in our lives. A well-balanced life directed toward day-by-day happiness can undoubtedly profit from doing something without seriousness, without responsibilities, without consequences.

We realize that most of our lives are filled with the necessities of seriousness. We do not have to look far to see our need for caring for our families, earning a living, and discharging our responsibilities. These are serious matters. But somewhere along the line there should be an opportunity to lay these matters aside for awhile and play, yes, play. I am inclined to think that the more the play is like the carefree play of a child, the more benefit we will receive from it.

If we think of play as activity without serious intent, what can we expect to derive from such activity? The benefits may fall into a medical category, a philosophical category, or perhaps a psychological category, but for our purposes let us look at the results purely from a casual man-on-the-street point of view.

Here are some possibilities. Any given possibility or result will apply in greater or lesser degree to your life, depending on your own attitudes and life pattern. As you read through this list, picture a group of children on a playground sharing a game while a warm May sun shines down on them and a pleasant breeze riffles their hair. Visualize how each of the listed results apply to the children in the group.

Some possible results of their play may be seen as:

> increase in laughter
> muscular relaxation
> addition of new friends
> increased appreciation of enjoyment
> new ease of conversation
> easier physical movement
> addition of drama to life
> addition of excitement to life
> addition of vigor to life
> addition of anticipation of future games or activities
> increased readiness to rest and go to sleep

Look back over this list; notice that the word *laughter* is at the head of the list. This is no accident. Can you picture a group of children at play in silence? Not easily. And when you do, there is a sadness to the picture. The immediate question is, What has robbed these children of laughter? Who is forcing them into silence? We sense without thinking that the sound that accompanies play is laughter. This is significant.

A friend recently told me of her response to a series of problems which had besieged her. She mentioned several deaths of friends and members of her extended family over the past few years. She spoke of the experience of a personal lingering illness. She then said, "I felt that I was weathering all these storms quite well, but suddenly I became aware that I no longer laughed."

She went on to say that the loss of laughter was in itself a sadness to her, a personal loss of something which had formerly been a real part of her life.

I believe that she was experiencing what we all experience at times, a realization that certain periods of our lives are no laughing matters. Instead they are temporarily crying matters.

This is undoubtedly a normal discovery, a discovery that hits us as a terrible force in time of crisis, but if that sensation of life being a crying matter persists too long, it should be attacked vigorously like any other half-truth. For life is partially an experience of laughter, as surely as it is partially an experience of tears. The practical attitude is that laughter is worth fighting for since laughter contributes a type of release of emotion to our lives.

Few have totally missed the good feeling of being with other people who cause them to laugh, and they report that after a good visit punctuated by laughter, they feel noticeably better than they had felt previously.

There is an old saying that laughter is the best medicine. A number of sayings concerning laughter in order to be well appear in literature which was written in widely differing times. This indicates that throughout the ages laughter has been accepted as having a salutary effect on the human body.

Recent studies have been done which bear out these statements as a physiological fact. Norman Cousins in his article in *The Saturday Evening Post* tells of his own experiences during an illness. His doctors told him that he had one chance in five hundred of full recovery, and he determined to try laughter as one avenue of treatment.[1] Books and television programs which were funny to him were presented systematically. He laughed hilariously day by day and found to his delight that not only did he feel better but also he received reports of improvement in medical tests.

This report of improvement in a life situation because of laughter is far from an isolated one. If laughter can help in time of real illness, how much more can it add to our lives day by day when we are in good health. Laughter is worthy of pursuit; it is a good and enjoyable activity in itself, and laughter is a part of the total picture of play.

Laughter comes from people who are at ease and experiencing joy. This is what I think we should seek as adults, the feeling of joyful relaxation which comes from play. Proverbs 17:22 says, "A merry heart doeth good like a medicine." I want a merry heart, and I am convinced that the pursuit of this merry heart which can aid in our own healing as surely as an excellent medication according to this verse is well worth investigation.

I remember an experience when my children were very young. Charles Kent was four and Kimball was no more than fourteen months old. My husband had been away on a business trip, and I had been carrying the responsibility of the children by myself.

Elise, my neighbor's niece, was visiting from next door. In the course of a conversation she told me that she would like to babysit for me. With these extra two hands to help with the little children, we decided to go swimming and the four of us, baby and all, left for the Dad's Club pool which was nearby. Elise was caring for Charles Kent as I was playing with the baby in the pleasant pool. A few minutes passed as the baby splashed and I splashed about with him in the water. Suddenly I heard myself laughing in great unrestrained burst of joy. I can still remember the surprise that washed over me as I realized that after only a few minutes of play in the water my whole frame of mind had changed. I was no longer worn down with care. I was no longer tired. I was rested and happy, all because I had been playing for a few minutes. I have never forgotten that experience. I learned that when chores get too heavy and constant it is time to lay everything aside and go play for a few minutes. The waiting work is far less tedious and responsibilities are far less heavy when I return.

While almost everyone will agree with me in theory about the value of play, it may be something else to find the play activity which is best for you. Like the small child who says, "Mama, what can I play?" we need to ask ourselves, as well as the wisest friends we have, What can I play?

First, remember that the joyous play which creates the laughter of childhood involves movement and action. I think adults need to hold on to that aspect of childhood play in so far as we possibly can. If you have medical problems which rule out physical activity, that is a different matter, but for those of us who simply need to move around until our muscles become something more than bowls of jelly, it is time to look for vigorous action. Most doctors are prescribing more exercise for all of us, and the exercise can become a kind of play. Consider this list of possible play activities. Which ones seem to be something you could enjoy?

swimming
bicycling
walking
tennis
golf
calisthenics in groups
calisthenics to music
gardening
volleyball
basketball
handball
backpacking
camping
marching with a band

Any of these can become a form of adult play. If we have lost our taste for these types of activities, perhaps we need to ask, What would I think of a child who came to me and said, "I hate to play".

The very thought of such a child is sad. But I believe it is not as sad as the adult who has ceased to share the relaxed world of play until he is saying by his actions, I hate to play.

Some of the approximately seventy-four dictionary definitions of *play* mentioned previously contain expressions, such as "to move about briskly, to exercise or employ oneself in amusement or recreation, and to do something in sport which is not to be taken seriously." Isn't it lovely to consider moving lightly and quickly in an activity which we are not taking seriously? And here we stumble upon one of the wonderful side benefits of play. As we refuse to take an activity or game seriously, we also refuse to take ourselves seriously in that activity. Therefore, for a brief time, we are free of our own burdensome egoes.

The person who has a perfectly relaxed ego can forget his position or lack of position, his authority or lack of authority. He can walk into a room without expecting his place to be waiting vacant for him, for all places are the same. He can enter whatever spot is open and feel utterly at home in that spot. This is the wonderful attitude of the person who is playing without seriousness, who is relaxing his entire being even as a child relaxes.

For a mental picture of relaxation, visualize a bird flying just above a treetop over an autumn woods. See the gentle lifting and falling of his flight. What can you do to make you feel as he looks? What would make you so completely at ease, moving in your own medium, unconcerned about who may be watching, following your own unique way through the pathless sky?

His is the attitude we are seeking in our play. When we have found our own unique play, the play which fits our mind and our muscles, we will find ourselves tapping a new reservoir not only of enjoyment but also of mental and physical energy since energy is frequently a by-product of relaxation.

My husband is one-half Bohemian. His father spoke both the Czech language and German before he spoke English. My husband, during the past few years, has begun to look back with deep interest to his own origins. Together, he and I have taken a Czech language course. Then we began to learn of the national dances of Czechoslovakia. Together we saw the colorful costumes and then we enrolled in a course in Czech and German folkdances.

As we skipped and turned, skipped and turned in these folk patterns, I again found what I had already discovered with the swimming experience years before. I found that a physical activity in which there is no seriousness and no responsibility can bring long-needed laughter, merriment, and relaxation toward life.

Shared play can also bring a closeness between marriage partners, who too often have shared only responsibilities and hard work. It is a strange situation that in our culture a couple share wonderful experiences of entertainment and participation before they are married and then, too often as though some dark curtain has been drawn, they withdraw completely from play and entertainment activities into a world of hard work, financial problems, and seclusion. This should not be! Play can keep a sparkle in marriage forever. It may well be one of the most widely overlooked elements in many floundering marriages today.

We have been looking only at active play, but there is also sedentary play to be shared. Games of all types where there is no seriousness involved and little ego at stake offer an opportunity for a rediscovery of real merriment. Diversion, freedom from pressure, freedom to express an unconsidered opinion, these all are desired aims.

Here is a list of some sedentary or slower-paced activities

which may produce some of these effects. If you do not immediately think of them as play, try to put them into the mental context of play and say with the abandon of a child, This is what I like to play. Do you like to play some of these games?

> make a long-distance call to a friend who gives you
> a mental lift
> take a long slow walk
> start a new piece of needlework
> go look at an old house you love
> walk by a place where you were once very happy
> buy a food that is special to you
> organize your desk or address book and feel the rush
> of energy from accomplishment
> go visit with a little child who is anticipating a birthday
> or Christmas
> go out to breakfast before the city is awake
> listen to a record you enjoy while you sit in your favor-
> ite chair in your favorite robe
> go to a movie in the afternoon or after work
> make your Christmas list, whatever the season
> go shopping and look at everything that is beautiful
> play any table game you enjoy with a good friend

My typist on the first draft of this manuscript made an excellent and very helpful typographical error in the copy. She had typed as the first item on the list above, "make a long-distance call to a friend who gives you a mental life." She had substituted the word *life* for *lift* and, thereby, opened an entire new area.

Some people do give us a mental life. Others hold our life to a completely functional and physical level. The mental life is a life of thought and intellectual and cognitive considerations. It is also the life of the humor of words, ideas, and even puns.

The shaggy-dog stories come to my mind as an excellent example of mental play. If you are a shaggy-dog person, you well know that these stories get their name from the comparison of the matted hair of the shaggy dog and the equally matted and tangled unimportant details of the story. In fact the shaggy-dog stories are given the very formal definition of stories which are often long and involved, filled with unimportant incidents with an absurd or irrelevant punch line.

I once entered a contest for Shaggy Dogs. I did not win, but I created the two following bits of shagginess, and I am sure of one thing, they both qualify as being play in the sense that they are without serious intent.

Shaggy Dog I

The toad frogs sat in the shade and snapped wildly at every delicious, juicy bug. But there was one long-legged toad with a slender, elongated body who was without desire for the tasty fare. The other frogs marveled at his restraint and questioned each other, "Why does this friend with the elongated body have no yen for this refreshing diet?"

Suddenly one wise frog said, "I have found the answer. It is simple. It is a long toad that has no yearning."

Shaggy Dog II

The Kiker family lived in great contentment. They had no problems and no discord. Even the eldest, Grandpa Kiker, had no quarrel with the youngest, little Keeter Kiker. One day a great argument arose, however, over the family recipe for kippers—Grandpa felt that capers should by added, little Keeter said no. Grandpa won the decision, and the kippers were prepared according to the caper recipe. That is why Keeter Kiker kicked a keg of capered kippers.

(A low moan is the accepted response to a Shaggy Dog, so do be my guest.)

The mental and the more sedentary activities above qualify as play because they indicate changes of pace, but it is good to keep in mind the thought of action and bit by bit add more action to the life.

Play suggests joy as we think of children at play or of animals romping at play. Milton says in "L'Allegro," and we can feel the rhythm of play in his word, that the "young and old come forth to play/On a sunshine holiday." Mark Twain, in *The Adventures of Tom Sawyer*, observed that "play consists of whatever a body is not obliged to do."

Play is and has always been a part of our tradition, but we have been too quick to abandon it in actual practice. I believe we need it as a constant activity. Even as we attempt to encourage our children toward their life work, we need to give a thought to their life play for the health of their bodies and the serenity of their minds. I believe that our complicated, intense culture needs the release play provides.

Play burns up nervous energy and leaves in its place healthy, tired muscles and minds. These are keys to a good night's sleep that permit us to wake up singing in the morning.

Note

1. Norman Cousins, "One Chance in 500 to Live," *The Saturday Evening Post* (June, 1977), p. 52.

12

Believe There Are Solutions to Your Problems

How many of these statements can you agree with?

Worry is a thoroughly useless activity.
Worry is habit forming.
Worry is controllable.
Worry can be replaced by problem solving.
All worry indulged in after going to bed has irrational elements and is distorted by exhaustion and night anxiety.

If you can agree with all of these statements you are in a frame of mind to look squarely at worry and begin to erase it from your life. One of the biggest steps I ever made in the control of worry was the decision of the last principle listed, the one having to do with night worry.

I began to be aware that when I would lie down at night, I would frequently pick up some problem and begin to turn it in my mind. The problem may not have been monumental, perhaps nothing more than a time-scheduling problem or an anticipated responsibility. With the pressure of feeling that I should get to sleep added to the emotional pressure of darkness, and the magnified sounds of night, I would find myself building the worry into a threatening tower of uneasiness. Then, because I am inclined to seek solutions, I would force myself to come to some decision about the matter. The decision would always seem very sensible at night. In the morning, however, I would find I had inflated the problem out of proportion, and the solution often had very little to do with the actual facts of the event under consideration.

Because some problems were becoming bigger than reality, I made the firm decision, in the bright light of the day, that I would never attempt to make a decision at night. Strangely, once that position was taken, my mind cooperated by accepting my statement to myself, I refuse to worry about this tonight because any decision I make will be useless since it is colored by night tensions. In this way I have an answer ready for use before the pattern of worry can establish itself.

This is one technique for dealing with worry. Let's look at others. Let's also consider some dimensions of worry in order to better destroy it.

The term *worry* is such a part of our language that each person uses it to mean whatever feels natural to him. Here are some common usages of the word.

I feel worried (troubled)
I have a worry (problem)
He is a worry to me (a bother)
I am worried about what to do (need for a decision)
Don't worry me (annoy)
My worries have broken my heart (griefs)
I worry all the time (fret)
He is a worry (nuisance)

It is little wonder that we remain shrouded in our "worries" if our language is any indication of our confusion.

Perhaps when we use the word *worry* we are not clear as to what we are saying; we have not taken the time to put our concerns into categories where they can be managed. Until concerns are categorized and managed, they may hang around reaching destructive fingers into every day. If, however, we pinpoint concerns and decide what action must be taken, concerns may yield themselves to an early solution and removal from life.

In the list of stress or worry situations listed, select those categories into which your present concerns fall. In the space at the left of the list, place the word which indicates to you your specific worry in order that you can see at a glance where your worries are grouped.

    the need to overcome bitterness
    the need for more money
    the need to make a decision
    the need to change a habit
    the need to be rested physically
    the need to complete a task
    the need for human companionship
    the need for prayer
    the need for forgiveness
    the need for a new schedule
    the need to understand methods of dealing with grief
    the need for more comfortable living conditions
    the need to remove yourself from an unwholesome situation

Each of the areas of concern listed here could be indiscriminately listed as a worry, but once they have been labeled in such a general way we may have confused the issue. We may think of the concerns as some vague, impossible shadows which are pursuing us, rather than realizing that they are in fact specific needs which require specific solutions.

We might say that we are worried about our bitterness, but no progress will be made until we understand that what we need is the definition of some of the possible ways of attaining victory over bitterness. We may need a specific book on the subject, or we may need a talk with our pastors.

A need for specific action is present. There is no need for some general depression which we may call worry.

We may say that we are worried about our physical exhaustion; but until we clearly face the fact that we need to cancel some evening activities and get to bed earlier, we have not understood our problem. The need is for a specific rest and sleep schedule, not for a blurry feeling of worry about our drowziness.

We may say that we are worried about smoking. This is a general statement of distress which does not face the real need. The specific problem is the need for a method or a decision to seek help in breaking the smoking habit.

We may say that we worry because we don't have any friends. This issue is so much more easily dealt with when seen as a need to be more interested in other people or a need to widen our range of activities until they provide opportunity to meet new friends.

Worries are frequently specific needs rather than general fuzzy areas of discontent and uneasiness. The specific need responds to action, whereas the fuzzy uneasiness only lingers on, taking the brightness from the day and never arriving at a point of decision. First understanding your worry is necessary and, second, understanding how it can be removed.

At times our worries become so confused as to their real nature that they become comic. Consider the person getting ready to walk out the door to work in the morning. The sky is cloudy. The air feels damp. The day is threatening. The weatherman has said the day will be fair without any rain. Suddenly the person is faced with the dilemma of whether to carry an umbrella. He may say, "I am worried about whether I should carry an umbrella." This is not a worry; this is a simple decision. Either the person will or will not decide to carry the umbrella. There may be minor considerations involved, such as the umbrella may be an annoyance to carry later in the evening after work when the person is going out to dinner. There is the likelihood of losing the umbrella which is new and handsome. Or the umbrella may be a problem on the bus, where it is difficult to avoid jabbing other passengers. All of these things may be true, but the fact remains that the umbrella situation is no more than a question, requiring a decision.

Probably you will agree readily that this is a question and not an anxious emotional torment because the question is relatively unimportant, but look one step further. How many of your worries and mine actually fall into this category of a decision? We are wasting emotional energy on them. They are matters requiring clear thought because their results may cause consequences far greater than the simple problem of carrying a useless umbrella all day. However, if the only requirement is a decision with manageable consequences, we are confronted with a question which needs an answer and not an emotional burden.

It is an important step to separate decisions from a vaguely shaped mountain of emotion. A decision faces the worry. It says, This is no vague concern; it is an opportunity to decide between two possible actions. Action creates vitality, and my worry has now been understood as an opportunity for the vigorous activity of decision.

Sometimes what appears, at first, to be a worry or a problem is nothing more than a need for concrete information. This is a problem which usually can be solved without undue effort. Either some person, a library, a local place of business, or a professional person can supply the answer and we are free to move on. The need for an answer may have elements of tension in it. This is the reason the troubling question should be faced, accepted, and put on the priority list high enough to drive you to the telephone or reference book.

I remember a question asked by a child which made me

aware of the acute need for answers.

On March 18, 1959, President Eisenhower signed the act which accepted Hawaii as our fiftieth state. All day at school the children had said again and again to each other and to their teachers, "Hawaii is now a part of the United States."

The school day was over and the children came home, still full of the fact that this day had been a day which would be recorded in the history books. The thoughts of the events of the day formed a lively bit of conversation in my backyard when suddenly during a lull in the conversation a small voice said, "But, Mrs. Prokop, what I can't understand is how did they get it over here?"

My mind raced about wildly for a moment before I understood exactly what this eager and very intelligent little child was asking. Suddenly the sentence which the children had repeated formed itself in my mind—"Hawaii is now a part of the United States."

For a moment I had a vision of great ships slowly towing Hawaii to our West Coast. I even shared for a second the amazement which some Californians would feel as they stared from the windows of their beach homes to see Mauna Loa lifting its craters against the sky. Then I tried to explain to my little friend that Hawaii had not been moved physically.

I have thought of this question many times since that day, and I have wondered just how many times our children have failed to grasp the real facts in the great maze of information which they receive. I wonder even more how often adults stumble along worrying about a question when all we need is a simple answer.

Some decisions, as well as questions, unfortunately must be dealt with in crisis situations or perhaps in a tight time frame. These frequently take on added tensions, as well as added facets of confusion, and who would deny that tension is a common reaction; however, who also would deny that tension is a weakening and confusing reaction? We need to remember that the need for decision has frequently not changed as we plunge into confusion; it is only that the necessary decision is now surrounded by stress.

Let's consider a crisis situation in which a job has just been lost. This is a desperate reality for almost anyone. It is a crisis situation which is frequently surrounded by uneasiness and perhaps complicated by feelings of resentment and anger. While these things are true, the fact remains that this is a decision situation. The decisions which must be made are:

> How will I pay the bills until I am resettled?
> Where will I look for a job?
> Should I try to get more training before I apply?
> Whom shall I call?
> Will I accept a job outside my geographical area?
> What clothes will I wear to be interviewed?
> Is my resumé in order?
> What salary must I secure in order to pay my bills?

The fact remains just as firm that the person asking these questions is in need of a job, but the emphasis has been transferred from the wild shout, "I'm worried to death," to specific questions which will remedy the situation or at least begin to open doors toward an answer.

A similar situation involving a search for a job in a less, crisis-oriented atmosphere may be seen in a job-change activity which confronts many workers.

Perhaps the job holder has an adequate job which pays the bills and which is not too unpleasant. However, the employee realizes that the job has no opportunity for financial advancement or for increased skills. Another consideration is that the worker does not have time to do the things he would like most to do on his present schedule. Perhaps he even feels that he has a real calling to do another type of work. Perhaps he knows that he has certain abilities which are being wasted and which are slowly diminishing from lack of use.

An anticipated but ineffective reaction to this situation is to cry out, "I'm worried about my future." While this reaction may be expected from most of us, the fact remains that this is not a situation for the anxious, uneasy, fretful, or tormented responses. It is the time for decisions. This person needs to face questions which will bring him to a point of decision about the job. He may ask:

> Can I find a job in the field I want to enter which pays as much as my present job?
> Do I stand a chance of getting the job?
> Should I quit and look for another job?
> Can I hold up under the uneasiness of being temporarily unemployed?
> Should I try to look for another job in addition to staying on where I am?
> Should I try to find satisfactions in other activities in after-work hours and stay with the job I have?

The situation of this job holder is serious and real. It should not be minimized. The only observation is that this is a situation requiring decisions not a lifetime of fretting and trembling.

A good rule of thumb in life-changing situations might be that if we indulge in fretting without any action for as long as six months, we have probably not faced the fact that we are confronted with a need for decision. Instead we have substituted an emotional push and pull activity known as worry.

It is interesting that one of the dictionary definitions of the word *worry* is "to seize, especially by the throat with

the teeth and shake or mangle as one animal does another."
We could thus quite properly say that a dog was worrying
a bone. But how many problems have we all shaken and
mangled until in our minds they have become unrecogniz-
able masses? In this case it is time to drop them on the
ground until we are ready to pick them up, turn either
right or left, and either lay them down, or else go trotting
off with them to a new location.

Decision is the desirable word. *Mangle* is the undesirable
opposite in this case.

Beyond decisions, there are challenges which face us. We
may look at these challenges negatively and say, I am worried about my ability to do this. Much of this negative
approach can be erased when we realize that the everyday
movements of life are characterized by small changes which
carry with them a certain tension, a heightened awareness.
This is not bad. This is not a bugaboo to be sweated over.
This is life!

If we fight against the necessity to be alert, and even a
little tense over meeting the new director, having guests
in for dinner, or making a critical phone call, we are probably
attaching too much importance to the event. Meet the director; entertain the guests; make the phone call, and experience the little tension. Next time there will be less tension
and more enjoyment, and you can say, I have met a challenge and I have grown.

In addition to worries, which in fact are problems requiring a decision, there is another area of worry that besieges
most of us. This is the vague, threatening, philosophical
worry that comes upon us in the night, keeps us awake,
and destroys our effectiveness for the next day. This worry
is compounded of the big worries about all the starving
children of the world, the continuing inflation and unem-
ployment, the atomic wars, abuse and hatred, as well as
the energy crisis, and diminishing private enterprise. A defi-

nite attitude and philosophy must be adopted toward these because if we are to live with any serenity, we must handle these concerns.

First of all I would say, these considerations are real. They are important, they, with variations, are a part of the sadness men have experienced in all ages. Any person who has absolutely no concern about these things is scarcely worthy to be called human, much less Christian. And having said this, we move on to the next thought, What do we do about these haunting concerns?

First, whatever we can do to alleviate the suffering of a member of our neighborhood or our family, we need to do immediately. But once this is done, what is the next step?

Is the next step to go home and wring our hands because we have done so little and cannot do more? Frankly, if this activity brought glowing relief to the world, I would say, Yes, wring away; but the most simple reasoning assures us that there is no balm in hand-wringing.

An over-supply of emotion only serves to torment us into a state where we are totally unable to be a good companion, mother, father, neighbor, or employee. It soon becomes apparent that to be harried for a good cause is only slightly better than being harried for a useless cause. *Harried* is not an effective state of mind.

We all seem to carry about in us some of the old, dark superstition that if we just worry about things enough, they are bound to be helped. This falls into the category of refusing to enjoy a beautiful Christmas dinner because there are people who are hungry in India. It also fits into the category of telling a child to eat all the food on his plate because the children in Africa are hungry.

The point is, these events are simply not related. True, a child may need to eat all the food on his plate. True, there are hungry people all over the world and we should help them. But these two facts do not have any bearing on each other. If the child leaves food on his plate, the hungry children of other lands will not be affected. It is also true that there are people who are not enjoying a good Christmas, but the added agony of the person refusing to enjoy his day will not affect that sadness.

It is futile superstition to believe that if we keep ourselves in a constant state of anguish over certain situations, that anguish will someway hold problems in balance and make them less terrible. It is much like holding your mouth in a certain way to force a ball to strike the bowling pins. You may hold it there if you like, and many of us do, but the contribution toward success remains in doubt.

If anguish or posturing could accomplish anything, I feel we should advocate that we all get out with brochures and educational stations for instruction in the fine arts of grief performance. But the fact is that anguish is a defeater not an achiever. It may force its way into our lives at times, but it does not produce solutions. It is a wearying, futile activity that weakens possibilities for effectiveness. It is easy—but seldom helpful—to say, Don't sit around thinking about a problem you can do nothing about. But it is much more difficult for the owner of the problem to remove it from his mind. Worries just do not vanish because we tell them to.

God has a positive suggestion for replacing the negative problem. Where we are inclined to tell friends to remove the problem from their minds, God's Word tells us what to put in the vacuum left by removing the problem. "Finally, brethren, whatsoever things are true, whatsoever things are honest, whatsoever things are just, whatsoever things are pure, whatsoever things are lovely, whatsoever things are of good report; if there by any virtue, and if there by any praise, think on these things" (Phil. 4:8).

This is God's command for our thought pattern. If God

had given us the responsibility of holding the state of the world in balance by worry, Philippians 4 would read far differently. If worry were the solution, perhaps a verse would read, "Christian, worry constantly. Agonize and cry, tear your hair and the purposes of God will be brought about." How foolish this sounds! It is not God's way. Our God is a God of a sound mind, and he commands us toward sound practices.

Again, I return to the statement that these problems of the world are real. We should do anything we can to help alleviate suffering, but helping does not include worrying about the problems through the night and awakening to new terrors each morning.

In a sense we each have a given amount of energy to spend. That amount of energy may vary from day to day and year to year, but nevertheless we are dealing with something less than unlimited strength. If our supply of energy is spent on worry, what will the source of energy for solutions be? I believe that the logical system is to divert worry energy to solution purposes. The following examples are of people who had not considered this more positive use of their energy.

Recently a friend dropped by after work, drank a cup of coffee, and carried on a detailed description of the problem she had with her fingernails. They split, broke easily, and were a darkish color she said. When she started to describe how they separated into layers, I interrupted her with the question, "What do you plan to do about it?"

She stopped in amazement and said, "Why, I hadn't really thought about that. I was just thinking of how terrible they look." Surprisingly, she had never made a serious effort to improve her fingernails; she had only repeatedly analyzed the problem. All of her energy was centered in the problem not its solution.

Another friend, on several occasions, discussed her marriage. Her husband was inconsiderate, uncooperative, and even dishonest she felt. She went on to prove just how undesirable he was by telling me of a conversation in which he said "this" while she said "that."

After awhile I asked her the same question I had asked my friend who had the problem with her fingernails. "What do you plan to do about it?" She admitted that she had not ever seriously evaluated possible concrete solutions; she had only gnawed endlessly at every aspect of the problem itself.

A hard-working neighbor talked with me about her frustrating dreams for the future. Her present job was routine, but she dreamed of adventure. Her present salary was meager, but she dreamed of affluence. After I asked her about possible solutions to her problem, she admitted that she had never made one phone call, requested one brochure, or investigated one college catalog to find possibilities for improving her future.

While it is true that every problem must be considered and understood to a degree before it can be solved, it is equally true that if the problem becomes the real object of study while a solution is ignored, it is unlikely that a solution will ever be found. Any energy, either mental or emotional, which is spent on facets of the problem after it is once understood becomes simply a way of refusing to seek a solution. It becomes an activity in which energy is squandered by muddling about in the problem. You simply work with the problem rather than the solution.

Here are ten questions which may serve to help you discover whether you are still playing and worrying with your problem or are ready to embrace a solution.

Answer each question yes or no.

1. Can you state, in simple terms, three possible solutions to your problem?

2. Have you considered the possible consequences of the three alternate solutions?

3. Can you state, in one sentence, the solution which you would most like to see come about?

4. Do you have concrete plans for your activities for at least one week after your problem is solved?

5. Do you anticipate a definite improvement in your life as a result of your solution?

6. Do you talk with someone about the details of your problem at least twice a day?

7. Do you have friends with whom your principal area of mutual interest is your problem?

8. Do you think of your problem as a developing drama?

9. When you think of your problem, do you feel a desire to wait to see what happens next as contrasted with a desire to see a solution?

10. Do you experience a feeling of some importance because of your problem?

When you can honestly answer yes to the first five questions and no to the last five, you are investing your energy in seeking a solution. If you cannot answer the first five questions yes and the last five no, you are still squandering your energy on the problem itself and ignoring possible solutions. It is only through the pursuit of solutions that we can wake up singing.

13

Begin to Understand Happiness

Happiness is not the chief aim of life, but few would deny that it is a very wonderful by-product of living an effective, productive life.

The Bible speaks over and over of peace, joy, and contentment. Paul cries out from Philippians, "Rejoice, Rejoice!" Surely the pursuit of not only happiness but also a greater understanding of happiness is worth our time.

There are so many different types and degrees of *happiness* that a firm definition of the word almost escapes us. But let's think in terms of the dictionary synonyms of "pleased, glad, delighted, or contented."

The dictionary further dissects happiness and comes up with some beautiful words and thoughts, all of which are a part of the big portrait. A composite of several dictionary definitions yields up the terms *well-being, peace, state of enjoyment, satisfaction, bliss, comfort, joy, gladness, graceful felicity, fitness, cheerfulness, blitheness,* and *jubilance.* My thesaurus goes on to list as synonyms *fortunate, joyous, ecstatic, apt,* and *glad.* My reaction to all of these is, That's what I want!

Our hearts naturally pursue happiness. The smallest child or the most mature adult in most cultures evaluates the goodness of his days by the amount of happiness he has experienced. This may be the quiet contented happiness of having done a job well, or it may be the exuberant happiness of exhilarating play. Whichever it may be, it is still happiness. We all want to feel good about the things we are doing, about the people we are contacting, about the situations we are moving through, and certainly all of this is a part of our happiness.

However, I have come to believe that happiness is basically two things: It is an attitude toward life, and it is a benediction from God.

As in most everything in our Christian experience, there is a Godward side and a manward side; I believe that here we see man assuming an attitude or point of view toward life which partially determines his emotional state. If that view is hopeful, trusting, and peaceful, happiness results. If the view is despairing, faithless, and antagonistic, unhappiness results.

At the same time there is the Godward side which comes to man in the form of blessing. This result is shown in the promise, "Thou wilt keep him in perfect peace, whose mind is stayed on thee, because he trusteth in thee" (Isa. 26:3). This peace direct from God is, I believe, the ultimate happiness which can come to man.

Let's first consider happiness as an attitude toward life. Happiness is not a good job; it is an attitude about a job. A job which pays well and affords pleasant surroundings is certainly more conducive to happiness than one which pays poorly and is executed in miserable conditions. The same job may bring an element of happiness to one person and misery to another because of the difference in their attitude toward the job.

Happiness is not a good family; it is an attitude toward a family. This becomes evident when we listen to various people talking about their families. Some people find great happiness with their spouses and children; others find misery, and frequently there are few major differences in the characteristics of the families involved.

The secret is in the attitude, not in the events themselves. Again this is evident when we see happiness in conditions of sickness or happiness in conditions of need. It would seem that the happiness would be destroyed by either of these disasters, but it becomes clear that an attitude of faith or an attitude of trust may completely overshadow the events themselves.

Big exciting events may or may not cause happiness, and little insignificant events may or may not cause equivalent degrees of happiness. The emotion lies in the attitude toward them.

As a friend said recently, "I cleaned the refrigerator last night, and I've felt good all day just realizing how clean it is." For her, happiness was a clean refrigerator, but there are many other people who have cleaned a similar refrigerator and have sighed sadly because they were forced to deal with such a menial task. It cannot be escaped that the happiness or lack of it lies in the attitude toward the event.

As this thought is expanded from the realm of refrigerator cleaning to, shall we say, a trip to London, the situation remains the same. The happiness is not inherent in the refrigerator or in the trip to London. It lies in the attitude of the individual. Happiness, in its largest sense, is a joyful attitude toward life; it is a joyful way of looking at and of living life.

In addition to the attitude, I believe that God bestows happiness on our hearts, just as he blesses us in other ways. I cannot otherwise account for the sudden and unexpected rush of happiness and peace over the heart when there is no material explanation for it. Ralph Waldo Emerson in "Nature" made, what is to me, a startling yet totally understandable observation when he said, "Crossing a bare common, in snow puddles, at twilight, under a clouded sky, without having in my thoughts any occurrence of special good fortune, I have enjoyed a perfect exhilaration. I am glad to the brink of fear." I see such an experience of pure happiness as a direct blessing from God.

If happiness is then partially our own attitude and partially God's blessing, how can we discover consistent personal happiness and live in its reflection hour by hour?

I believe the answer is simpler than we may think. I believe this is the answer: Identify exactly those things (activities, events, people, and objects) which have in the past made you happy both spiritually, physically, and mentally and then pursue those things with all your being in so far as your good judgment (shaped by prayer and realistic thought) and your life pattern permit.

There are two reasons for this statement far beyond a mere mad pursuit of pleasant or exciting events. They are the following:

1. These identified things (activities, events, people and objects) are the things toward which you are capable of holding an attitude of joy.
2. These identified things (activities, events, people and objects) are the things in which God has bestowed his blessing of happiness in the past.

This principle may be summarized as, Where you have walked well in the past, in perfect blessing, attempt to walk again daily.

I feel that God's guidance frequently is revealed in the great happiness which we experience in doing certain things. I believe that he reveals to us the abilities and the aptitudes he has placed in us and he encourages us to use and develop them by granting great happiness as they are used. As an example, a man may experience great joy in painting because he is using that gift God has placed in him. He is led by happiness into that area where God has provided a gift. The happiness he experiences is God's benediction on the talent God has created, as well as a part of God's guidance toward further use of his gift.

At one time our son went through an extensive testing program for the purpose of seeing exactly where his abilities lay. The tests included everything from idea flow to the grip strength of his left hand. In the evaluation period following the tests, the psychologist remarked that people usually want to do and seem led toward those fields in which they have the greatest competence. I think this is true psychologically and spiritually. God leads us through the happiness of accomplishment which attends those activities in which he has enabled us to function.

Before going on to discover those things which do bring happiness to our lives, we must stop to answer one startling question which springs to mind. Do you mean that I should do whatever makes me happy, regardless of its consequences?

My first answer would be that if this question springs wildly into your mind, bringing with it pictures of grand escapades which you have scarcely dared to dream of, you are probably confusing the concepts of long-term happiness with short-term thrills.

If the imagined source of happiness would ultimately be destructive to yourself or to others, the chances are that you have not evaluated the matter wisely. You may be thinking in terms of excitement for today rather than of contentment for a lifetime. Obviously the long-term happiness and contentment is what we are thinking of. Charles once told our son that if he were looking for intense excitement, it was hard to beat being chased by a raging bull; but if he were looking for happiness, he would probably find it entirely outside the bull's pasture. This seems to contrast the two situations quite accurately.

Look back to the question, what has made you happy? Do you honestly know? As an exercise to discover your sources of happiness in the past think back and list the ten happiest days of your life, as you remember them.

Complete your list before continuing with the following questions.

Look back through your list and recall the following for each day:

> What events happened on these ten days?
>
> Were these events characterized by personal relationships or happenings?
>
> Were they quiet or active days?
>
> Were they days of expectations or of fulfillment after long waiting?
>
> Were they in beautiful surroundings or ordinary settings?
>
> Were the best part of the days experienced in the morning or later parts of the day?
>
> Were they in settings of extreme order or disorder?
>
> Were they beginnings or endings?
>
> Were they carefully planned events or surprises?
>
> Were they final closings of long endeavors or sudden completions of activities?
>
> Were they in casual or formal settings?

As you answer each of these questions honestly, you will doubtlessly begin to see a pattern emerge. You will see that you have been happy in quiet, beautiful places with carefully planned events or perhaps you will see that your happiest days have been when you were surprised by joy by people or events and that places had no bearing on the situations.

I speak of the necessity for honesty in making these observations because your choices will probably indicate those things which make you happy not only today but ten or fifty years from now. These tendencies are deep within us, rising from we can only guess what combination of genes, early life experiences, and consciously self-taught principles, but they are here to stay. They are consistent from hour to hour and year to year.

Many of us seem to enjoy essentially the same type of things at two years of age as we enjoy at fifty. For this reason it is probably futile to attempt to change the enjoyment areas radically. True, we may need to shape and refine them in order to fit in harmoniously with our families and friends. But a complete denial of their existence can lead only to frustration and loss of good fruitful days.

I found long ago that my happiness flourishes best on a firm foundation of peaceful, unhurried days spent with stimulating people. A sense of accomplishment is necessary for my day to be exuberant. I understand perfectly Ernest Hemingway's "death loneliness" which he says comes at the end of a day that is wasted. I may spend days in many good and worthwhile activities, and I may overschedule my time, but I know that at the end of those days I will come up vaguely ill at ease. Intense, closely scheduled activity is not my path to happiness, even though I may applaud intense activity in another's life.

I have friends who have totally different patterns of happiness. Lovely parties and luncheons scheduled between numerous apointments create a good full day for them. I hasten to say *neither their situation of happiness nor my situation of happiness is better or worse than the other.* There is simply no value judgment involved. The widely differing patterns simply *are.* I am bound by mine, and they are bound by theirs. The point is, and must be, if we are to find happiness, we must objectively discover what our specific happiness pattern is.

After the discovery of our happiness pattern, the second discovery must be that of how we can spend a maximum number of days in that type of activity which brings happiness to us. The third point must be (and I hasten to add this before we jump to the conclusion that this must be a selfish activity which rules out all other needs and desires) how can we handle this pursuit in such a way that it does not take away from the happiness of those whom we love and around whom we live.

True, I love a quiet rainy day but why magnify it, especially to the point of offending my friends who hate quiet rainy days. The fact that I am by birth, training, and experience an introvert with an extroverted mouth and pencil is of limited interest to anyone else. I love my friends with a deep undying loyalty, but I must have time alone to think and work.

When the dark rainy season closes in on Houston, which is home to me, I usually get a call from a friend who says, "I just called to tell you that I know you are over there purring like an old cat, with a cup of tea on your desk, a sharp pencil in your hand, and a tousled afgan over your feet." He then adds, "Just remember that I am out here dull and depressed with cold coffee in my cup, my typewriter mildewed, and my feet itching in wet shoes."

Sun or shade, rainy days or fair, snowy mornings or sun rise in the tropics, whatever it may be you respond to, this is just a little part of that big something which could be called settings for life. The science and art of discovering exactly which of these makes you personally and individually happy is a part of effective living. Once the discovery is made, the genius is in slowly and methodically moving toward that destination of greater happiness. It is a long-recognized fact that you will probably arrive at the destination you choose, so make your decision carefully. Seldom, or only by accident, do any of us hit those things at which we are not aiming. If we aim for happiness, we are much more likely to hit it than if we aim indiscriminately at whatever may be moving on the horizon.

Your considered answer to the question of what makes you personally happy may cause changes in your life. Some of these changes may be in your daily schedule, to include or exclude certain activities, to change the use of your free time and vacations to include those things you have admitted are important to you. You may decide to change some personal habits to make the best use of the time of day in which you are happiest or to change something about your appearance in order to look more like the person you are when you are at your happiest. You may make changes in your usual guest list to include those people with whom you can share steps toward happiness or you may arrange your furniture to better serve the life you enjoy.

Changes may be drastic, or they may be minor. The prize at the end of all the effort is your own glowing days of happiness, a deep satisfying happiness. This kind of happiness causes you to say at the beginning and end of each day, "I am glad that I am alive today. I love to live. I am a happy person. Thank you, God, for life."

Happiness builds on itself, even as anger and bitterness feed on themselves and grow accordingly. This is the reason casual, unthinking acceptance of unhappiness, with no real thought toward change, is so dangerous. The person who gets off on a binge of singing "Rainy Days and Mondays Always Get Me Down" may find the downs intensified with each rainy day and Monday. There is only despair at the end of such negative pursuit.

On the other hand, the individual who daily evaluates his happiness and calls his joys by name is building a tower of awareness of personal happiness and intensification of every experience of happiness. He is writing a textbook of happiness to which he can return for a constant refresher course in joy. He can recall the joy of morning coffee on the patio and the sudden realization that five friends have called this week to say, "Have you read . . . ?" or "Have you thought . . . ?" He can recall little joys, even as I can recall when five-year-old Nicole came and wriggled in to share my chair while I was chairing a meeting in her mother's den. Why did she come? Just because she wanted to, and that is what makes it a joy to remember.

As we pursue and embrace happiness, a surprising question emerges. It is, Will we be able to accept happiness? The immediate and seemingly obvious answer is, "Why, of course." But this is not always the situation. The heart that has lived with unhappiness too long may feel uncomfortable and guilty in the presence of happiness. There is sometimes a deep, unexamined, superstitious thought that there is some reward due for suffering and some punishment attached to happiness. To the unhappy person, the old sadnesses are dark; but they may have become rather dear and familiar since they present no new or unsettling thoughts. As someone once explained her life, "I am living in hell, but at least I know the names of the streets." There is a deep truth here which cannot be ignored. Changes, even from despair to happiness, require courage. But as hard as it may be to face the changes and gain the strength for victory, it remains that courage is still the best event in town; the open heart can learn to embrace it.

I am constantly held by Paul's statement, "I know both how to be abased and how to abound" (Phil. 4:12). Paul put equal emphasis on his ability to be abased and to abound. Strangely, we are prone to attach virtue to suffering well and give little praise for flourishing well. I believe we are missing something. We need to abound with skill and well-being. And yes, when the abasement comes, we'll try to deal with that also, but abounding is the part we relish most.

In college I stumbled upon a truth regarding abounding that has remained with me. I learned that if I could not abound and be happy today, there was little reason for thinking I would be abounding and happy tomorrow. This thought placed the challenge on today. Tomorrow brings no magic in its dawn; the magic lies in the heart that observes the dawn. Happiness, like charity, begins at home; home, in this context, means deep inside the individual where he is himself and where he truly lives. This is contrasted with happiness lying outside ourselves, where some great performance or series of events in under way.

I hope I have persuaded you that I am sold on happiness as a way of life, because I am completely sold. And then because I am so convinced of the value of happiness I want to present the opposite side of the coin. The side that says, "OK, I agree with you, but I am still unhappy at times, regardless of my conviction about the possibility and desirability of happiness."

My feeling here is that some unhappiness in life is to be expected and anticipated. When it comes it can be accepted with, if not happiness, at least equanimity and grace. It is neither a spiritual nor an emotional failure to experience low periods as well as highs, and the person who never admits that the two emotions exist in his life is carrying a needless burden. I have come to believe that periods of slight depression which come for short periods are a part of life on this earth. They may arise from a physical basis, an emotional basis, from events which strike too quickly to permit mental orientation, or from stress. These dark periods do not represent failure in living; they represent a response to the change and uncertainty of life's process.

Even in this advanced age of medical progress, little is known of the precise workings of the mind, its need for rest, its need for change of pace, or its need for revitalization. Sleep experts have not even been able to determine as yet exactly what the recuperative process of sleep does for the mind. Is it a rebuilding of cells or a relaxation of muscle or something entirely different? In view of our lack of knowledge of our minds, I do not rule out that the renewal of mind and emotion, the downs which follow the emotional highs, are another of God's marvelous provisions for preserving the fragile texture of our mental processes.

When we think of the sustained mental and emotional excitement of the holiday season, so often followed closely by the low period of exhaustion and listlessness, we see a natural healing and revitalizing process at work. Perhaps the January slowdown is only a reaction to physical overactivity, but it is probably much more. Probably it is the much-needed rebuilding period.

God created our fabulous bodies which are so intricate that medical science can little more than guess at their potential. One of the evidences of their grandeur is their admitted ability to rebuild themselves. A limited degree of unhappiness and a desire for quiet retreat from normal movement may well be a part of the rebuilding process. However, excessive periods of either depression or unhappiness, demonstrate that something is amiss.

Beyond the slight periods of unhappiness which seem to follow high periods of excitement, even as the night follows the day, there are periods of vague sadness which come unexpectedly with a quiet darkness. They leave us as mysteriously as they have come.

These periods come to many people late in the evening as the twilight engulfs the earth. They might well be called twilight-despair. There are few people who would not understand something of what this term suggests. There is frequently with this feeling an emotion of homesickness and of a yearning for places long abandoned.

I have come to believe that there is a great deal more involved in these yearnings than the mere experiencing of the dying day. It may be that in this period of deepening twilight we are recalling our identification with the race of men of which we are so small yet so respected a part. Perhaps in such moments God is reorienting us to our place in the great span of centuries, of lives and deaths, of mornings and evenings from Eden forward.

I am utterly convinced that everything in the Christian life has a meaning and a significance. Although we may never understand more than a fitful smattering of what is meant, still the thoughtful mind contemplates and searches, knowing that our God created no futile mechanism.

With this in mind, we recognize that God may have put within us an apparatus for deep soul identification with him, as we retreat back into a quiet feeling which is almost sadness as the day dies. Perhaps the emotion is actually remembrance and wonder. Perhaps it could best be evaluated by its depth rather than by its component parts. Perhaps it is memory and also anticipation of entrance into the night with God who is our companion through all nights. Perhaps it is preparation to enter the last night with God. All of this may be a part of the twilight-despair, and perhaps if we look again, it will not be twilight-despair but rather quiet twilight-anticipation.

There are so many kinds and stages of happiness. There is the peaceful happiness of the complete walk with God. There is the jubilant happiness of great good fortune. There is the thankful happiness of survival of great strain. There is the poignant happiness of the remembrance of good days. There is the hopeful happiness of the reach for tomorrow. There is the contented happiness of the hour of rest.

Each is different. Each is worthy of the search. Each is a gift of God. "Happy is that people, . . . whose God is the Lord" (Ps. 144:15). Each of these types of happiness is doubtlessly covered in this verse. Each happiness brings singing to our lives.